Radiation Sickness

by

Lama Milkweed L. Augustine Ph.D

authorHOUSE®

AuthorHouse™
1663 Liberty Drive, Suite 200
Bloomington, IN 47403
www.authorhouse.com
Phone: 1-800-839-8640

First published by AuthorHouse 7/19/2007

ISBN: 978-1-4343-1752-0 (sc)
ISBN: 978-1-4343-2155-8 (hc)

Library of Congress Control Number: 2007905161

Printed in the United States of America
Bloomington, Indiana

This book is printed on acid-free paper.

For myself,
And for all fellow victims of
radiation sickness,
for all of my fellow terminally ill.
God bless you all.

manipulates the easily viewed courage that dwells there within him, and without consciously trying, captures the hearts of everyone he sees and talks to. This man has suffered tremendously and atrociously as the victim of unrelenting agony of his severe radiation sickness that cannot be cured, as well as it's devastating affects, which herald horrific physiological damage as well as damage to the brain. However "Nuke" Wilcox has most undoubtedly enlightened the psyche, collective in nature, of the "Department of Energy," and the whole nation, as this one special story one is about to hear is most certainly one that is filled with appalling greed, cover-ups, court cases, and numerous fragments of lengthy interviews with the national media, the "Department of Energy," and even some of the Officials from the nuclear power plant, who still attempt with an ignorant fervor, to cover up what has happened, as they claim such arrogance that they feel no need or desire to settle anything, and never mind restitutions for the family of this victim who has happily worked for them since he received his license by the age of twenty. Yes, this young man never asked for anything, but for the chance to work in the plant as for what he had been trained to do, and handling nuclear waste was the one thing "Nuke" had been told to do, as his job had not altered since he began working there; he never once complained, nor had he asked for a higher and more "meaningful" position. To place it bluntly, the power plant Officials never attempted to let anyone really see why this happened, but very soon they were discovered. The outline of the nuclear accident will most certainly affect everyone who has a heart beating inside of them, as the ones who are truly responsible for this unspeakable tragedy and misfortune to truly comment, as well as to simply admit they made a mistake.

Again, this is a true story.

The Author, Lama Milkweed L. Augustine H.H. Ph. D
Jan, 21, 2007

Chapter One

BEFORE THE STORY FIRST began, it must be told about the man, but before that, the boy. "Nuke" Wilcox was a simple child born to a caring and highly ethical couple named Cellia and Jake Wilcox there in Tennessee. The boy was one who was quiet and very peace loving who respecting his parents as well as the religious values which he had been lovingly taught to him over the years. However he always carried a fascination with all things nuclear, but he did not believe in warfare or the use of unethical tactics and behaviors in nuclear science, etc, but rather, "Nuke" was simply a boy who was more an intellectual than anything else, but like all kids while growing up, he loved to play and had many friends who were drawn to his gentle and nonthreatening personality.

He attended school here in town and was very shy with girls, but they were attracted nonetheless. He was an only child, which meant that "Nuke" received all of they're undivided attention, as well as nurturing the wondrous talents that harbored inside him, which not surprisingly, science was his redundant subject as well as math, but the former he was better educated, and the boy still in the home, studied books and manuals of anything pertaining to nuclear physics, atomic theory, nuclear engineering, the way power plants work, and nuclear materials, and anything else having to do with this fascinating subject. He received high honors in school since he was in junior high, and his father was now buying him genuine college level books about this subject which they're son loved in a very peaceful manner. The boy's lifelong dream was to work in the "Sequoyah" nuclear power plant, which stood only three miles away from where they lived.

"Nuke" studied and studied in between his normal schooling and still received wonderful grades, as his parents were very proud of him. The young boy, now with the nickname "Nuke," as he was also called this by his parents, and eventually by the rest of the family, was still very shy and quiet, but he loved to talk to people nonetheless as he had many friends and companions who shared their time with him whenever he could. Fortunately "Nuke" lived only a mile or so away from the high school, so he walked there instead of taking the bus, hence he was in good health, or he rode his bicycle and locked it to the rack on school grounds.

Everyone knew "Nuke" would be working at the power plant someday, as even his teachers became enlightened when they saw him reading and reading and going over and over again through these seven to eight inch thick books of nuclear sciences and nuclear theory, and atomic theory, etc, as he was still well able to keep up his grades to a perfect A during his whole four years of high school.

There was one very specific time at the end of his final school year, and he was taking atomic science as he had done this during his four years, and his male teacher who had gone to "Stanford University" studied the same subjects "Nuke" had already been since he was thirteen. He genuinely appreciated "Nuke's" genuine brilliance and asked him to go to the head of the class, or to the blackboard, and he instructed the teen, only seventeen, to explain to the class what all nuclear power plant reactors have in common. "Nuke" was not nervous or shy about this assigned task, but he was still very humble in character as all of his fellow classmates fixated on this young teenager who was practically a Professor by now as he had a school wide reputation of what he was going to be, his likes, etc, etc. The gentle young teenager took the chalk in his right hand and walked up to the board and explained very depthfully, but in brief as well, so as not to take up the entire time, and talked in a manner in which his fellow peers could comprehend, as the commonality of all nuclear reactors, including the discussion of proton rods in the most used type of reactor in this country and the world, were depicted to them in such a way that unknowingly, this was to be on a test the following week. It was after class, which was the final one of the day, so everyone was going home, but "Nuke" and his teacher had a conversation about what he had just done. "Nuke," being very humble, spoke softly to begin with, but he appreciated what his teacher had to say, by which was in praise to his scholarly intellect that people his age rarely have obtained, even though some may be highly intelligent like "Nuke." His teacher inspected the huge book, which was a 3rd level college edition, and was the exact copy of the one his teacher had used in "Stanford." He was happy that "Nuke" earned the scholarship to go to a special University where he will receive the training he will need and the essential knowledge to work in the nuclear world. Again, being very humble, "Nuke" walked away with his head lowered and looking back to the kindly praise his teacher had given him, as even his fellow students had not hated him because of his brilliance, but were rather drawn to him in a good way, and not to use him to get what they want or need from an academic perspective.

The boy was highly intelligent as he was kind and warm. He was respected and was surprisingly serene. "Nuke" managed to receive a scholarship for the University as he had hoped would happen so he could receive his Degree in nuclear science and technology. "Nuke's" parents remember him as happy and excited but was nervous about leaving home for a period of at least three years, but during the summers, would return for the needed vacation. Again, he was recalled affectionately as the redundant subject amidst his memory during that period of his life was love.

"He was a very quiet and gentle young teen; when you had him fro a friend, you had him for life." ,expressed his father passionately.

"Nuke" barely struggled through his three years of college, because he already studied relentlessly the various subjects pertaining to nuclear materials, power plants, weapons, and of course, atomic structures and theory, and nuclear theory, as well as physics, but it was how nuclear power plants are run and their various structures and reactors, etc, etc. He was often lonely, however, as his scant letter writing to his parents revealed, as they spoke of only the task of intensive studying and the joy over what he's so far learned, and so on. The personality of the teen was changing, but not into something that would be unrecognizable to the parents or to anyone else who knew him. Rather, it was something that became a bit on the subdued side, as "Nuke's" words testified unintentionally that he was becoming more quieted from having not the opportunity to really mingle with his fellow students. The teen was so intent on working at the power plant back home, that apparently nothing else really mattered enough to make him temporarily break the cycle of hard work and mind blowing study and note taking, as he passed test after test with flying colors. In only a matter of eight weeks, "Nuke" made it to the Dean's and Chancellor's list, and he was called into their offices personally to talk with them.

"Nuke" remembers that he was as nervous as he was humble, that he could barely say his heart felt thanks, especially because of his withdrawal from his peers.

Nuke was a tall and very thin young man of six feet tall, and weighing in at only one-hundred and forty pounds, but soon lost much of it during his intensive studies at the University, which made him go down to just over one-hundred pounds. This terrified his parents as it had the school, but Nuke was harboring a deepening depression that he had no tangible idea existed, but it was all due to being so lonely as to why he sank even further in the world of academia. He was classified as the most brilliant student the "University of Tennessee" had ever seen in their midst, but again "Nuke" Wilcox was not in the least bit interested. What was found amidst this time period concerning his extreme humility was the fact of his profound religious upbringing as the deeply devoted Catholic he really was, as he seemingly distained from drinking both on and off campus, as this made him more unpopular, and most considered "Nuke" to be a Professor's pet, or a real "egg head." This hurt 'Nuke," and he only went into himself further, but still no matter what transpired here and abroad, nothing could remove the realistic faith from the volatile, but stabilizing soul of this young man.

The young man, now aged twenty, graduated from college, but before that, he took the mandatory testing at the office of the "Department of Energy" and passed as he got every question correct. A letter of congratulations was accompanied by the results of his testing, which numbered at least five-hundred questions, which included essay questions.

Again, although excited, the young man was humble and quiet.

Chapter Two

CELLIA AND JAKE WILCOX, who are "Nuke's" parents, have never forgotten how they're son has enriched they're lives which is far from a consequential level "Nuke" has always fascinated them easily with his "wondrous" energy and loving compassion that was seemingly endlessly directed at family, but at the very same time, yearning for the nuclear power plant in the horizon as he kiddingly said it "speaks out his name."

This young man who goes by the name of "Nuke" finally received his dream, which was beginning with the handling of nuclear waste, which his parents were very disapproving of. However, they knew there was no arguing the young man out of it, as this was the beginning of his career and they did not want to stand anywhere in his way of achieving that. However there was something rather odd, which his parents noticed, especially where his father has a friend from the Department, because the plant officials retained him in the restricted area where the huge waste containment rooms were located, and the employees here had to wear lead lined suits, special goggles, gas mask, and a contamination badge, as well as they must use geigercounters to frequently monitor the amount of nuclear radiation here. However nothing of this nature seemed to scare they're son as he would come home each day and tell them about the "fun" he had. Again, the officials who hired him never thought, despite his brilliance, that he was really good enough to work in the reactor areas or monitoring sectors of the plant, but at the same time, after a passing while, they finally spoke to Nuke about having him return to the University to receive another Degree so he would be completely qualified in all areas of running a nuclear power plant, but surprisingly he declined. Yes, Nuke declined, because he only wished to work here, and what was asked of him didn't at all really matter. Nuke said to them, "I just love being here, and working with and transporting waste doesn't bother me at all." However his father was also greatly worried about this task which his son has accepted. His mother also was quite shaken up regarding they're son handling nuclear waste every day.

Nuke kept a secret from his parents, however, as he later revealed in an interview following his accident involving the spill of nuclear waste. The secret was, he had been exposed daily to a very small, but safe, amount of nuclear radiation since he was the age of twenty years old, which was as soon as he entered this power plant. He decontaminated himself every day, as all employees are required to shower and to be exposed to geigercounters upon leaving the final gate of the plant. His medical files were censured so no one would know that he was being exposed, but Nuke knew he was, but refused to worry somehow, as this is where his religious belief comes in, as Nuke believed everything will be all right and that no tangible harm would come to him as this eventually stymied his parents who loved him so deeply, as neither one of them could fully comprehend the tender affection "Nuke" felt for not only power plant, but for the whole "nuclear" profession.

Yes, Nuke still managed to acquire his position at the power plant despite his declination of wanting to return to the University as he was instructed. Once more, and as earlier said, his parents worried excessively about his overall health as he was still, on an almost daily basis, being exposed to what nuclear power plant officials call, "safe" levels of radiation, but it was because of the young man's father, a foundry worker and machinist, Jake Wilcox, notified his personal friend who had been a school chum, but stayed in touch, and informed him of what was insidiously happening to "Nuke" as this man who was notified by the concerned parent was a member of the "Department of Energy." His friend from the Department agreed right away that this was not right and potentially dangerous as it is fatal, but he relayed to Jake that radiation exposure does happen on occasion to the employees in places as these. Again, the friend of Jake, or the parent of Nuke, spoke to the officials for the "Sequoya" plant there in Tennessee. They again covered up everything with shallow lies that caused the Department to swallow or to believe, as they began paying off some of the employees so they would not reveal this information that happened to leak from tight security. However officials responsible for the covering up of files, especially those pertaining to "Nuke," were confiscated and replaced with seemingly bogus ones to fool the Department, which was discovered much later after the terrible accident. But according to most of the plant's leading officials, employees like "Nuke" do not really matter quite as much as the technicians, and those who run and watch this complex equipment what makes a power plant run efficiently, but effectively and safely. But this certainly should make absolutely no difference, as all employees; no matter what job they perform in places like these their safety must never be compromised. But despite all of this back and forth battling with Jake and the "Sequoya" power plant, Nuke never once attempted to combat anyone or to even speak with anybody on the board of officials about his constant daily regimen of low does nuclear radiation exposure since he first arrived, as he equally never once desired, nor had thought of getting the "Department of Energy" in on things here. Secretly, Nuke was angry at his father for doing this, but although he contained brilliance, which easily won him every right to work anywhere in the nuclear industry, he refused to see those particular truths that would end up either discouraging him, or removing him from what he has dreamed about all of his life. This kind and gentle man was surely someone who merely and only desired to do whatever is asked for him and nothing more. This was an attribute which revolved avidly around him as it was copiously viewed by even those leading plant officials, hence nothing further consisting of consequence was found out as they soon realized the allegations had come form the man's parents and not from Nuke.

This perplexing, but simple situation had actually caused the whole family to worry; all that is but "Nuke." The man went joyfully to the power plant every day to handle deadly, unprocessed liquid nuclear waste as was trained both in the University, an on the job training while here at the plant during his four month trail residency. He was taught specifically how to be safe as well as just how to handle these fatal materials in both a proper and responsible manner.

Through all of this things finally calmed down at home as well as here at the plant, but this was mainly due to Nuke's parents finally pulling back they're interrogative and adamant opposition over the situation of this low level exposure, but the parents were still terribly unnerved about this said exposure. Amidst this parental brigade, Nuke made many friends here as even highly paid technicians truly expressed their appreciation over what this young man did on a daily basis to maintain a safe environment for everyone here, as well as all of those out there beyond the walls of this place which gives everyone electricity miles around. Nuke received much emotional and situational support from his increasing number of friends who became steadily closer as time here at the power plant passed. The all enjoyed this quiet man's innocent smile, his peaceful voice as it was accompanied by equally peaceful acts, but to most of the power plant officials, he was truly considered as a "push over," because "Nuke" never once made the slightest attempt to stand up against them, as he seemed to always somehow blame himself for his insidious misfortune.

Time had gone by here and Nuke remained handling this highly radioactive nuclear waste as he transferred it in eight gallon barrels, one by one, on heavy industrial hand trucks to the appropriate vehicles that came to the plant at least once monthly, as they took it away to either be recycled, or properly processed to make it more into the category known as low "rad" waste, or simply low level waste, and finally dispose of it carefully and responsibly by highly trained personnel as it is often buried in stable geographical areas which is mostly of sand. With a geigurcounter clutched in his glove clad hand, "Nuke" carefully inspected the specialized area at the back of the plant, as well as when he entered inside of these gigantic sized rooms constructed of heavy concrete and lead, and there are signs everywhere with the familiar "wheel" symbolizing anything radioactive or nuclear, which warns the personnel of potential contamination, radioactivity, or of anything else pertaining to all things "nuclear." "Nuke" most certainly truly loved what he was doing here and his status on the ladder of employees and their opportunities didn't at all seem to matter to him, as his humility was easily seen by everyone. He thought back to all of those past years, even as a child, how he studied and studied to get to where he is today, which had much included how satisfying it all really was to every part of him as it all had an incredible impact in his inner life. Nuke was peaceful here in this place of potential terror with a capital "T," which his truest of companions found incredibly hard to understand, especially where this particular environment, aside from the reactors, is the most dangerous element. However Nuke only went silently and happily about his daily business as even the heaviness of these specially designed suits that are lead lined, and sometimes equipped with a respirator, whenever applicable, was worn over his tall, thin body in an avid manner. "The suit never bothered me." ,Nuke calmly expressed his statement to the press.

The peacefulness which young "Nuke" experienced, now the age of twenty-four, was the simplistic joy of his literal lifelong dream that had never once begun to lose it's intensity, the process of achieving it, as well as the customary novelty when he began this line of work four years earlier. The "Sequoya" nuclear power plant was like a second home to this simple, but brilliant young man who writhed in humility, but he still continued to mingle freely with his many good friends which he has easily acquired along the way.

Chapter Three

NUKE AGED FORTY YEARS old and had gained quiet a lot of experience under his belt, so to speak, as this kind and highly intelligent man remained perched here in the waste containment areas of the plant. However when asked by the press about how his parents later felt regarding they're capable son working here all of these years since graduation, they simply said this:

FATHER, JAKE WILCOX; "After time passed and we realized Nuke was going to be all right, then Cellia and I decided to lay off with questioning him about his safety. But still, nonetheless, we both worried about his welfare, especially where we are his parents, and we know that regardless of how dangerous his work is, we cannot stand in the way of our son's right to fulfill his desires and dreams."

MOTHER, CELLIA WILCOX; "Like Jake, I worried extensively about Nuke's health, but he was not showing any type of adverse symptoms from being there all of this time. So like my husband, I too decided that I cannot stand in the way of our son's progress in his career. I have always worried secretly all during his growing up life, if Nuke would really benefit from working in an incredibly dangerous place like a nuclear power plant."

Nuke Wilcox had sustained many friendships here as well as respect for never obstructing any work at the plant, but one thing was rather odd as it was misconceiving, and that was that Nuke was suddenly asked to transfer the waste to the specially equipped transport vehicles alone and without another individual to be there in case of accidents, which included equipment failure and radiation leaks. According to some of Nuke's closest companions, this truly bothered them and they wanted to bring this up to the board of leading officials, but were claiming to always be "too busy" to comment or to meet with. The atmosphere here suddenly slowly became tense, which was certainly a prelude to something not good, but Nuke was completely and blissfully unaware of any of this that had been transpiring around him all of these weeks. Nuke was calm as he recalled, and enjoyed very much working with the waste, as he was the most comfortable of all of the employees who worked in this restricted area of the power plant. Everyone else told Nuke that they were always afraid to be there, but they also well understood that it must be taken care of, and the personal bills at home will not get paid otherwise.

Nuke became more quieted and subdued from the human environment at the power plant. He came home each evening with a sad look on his long, thin face, and often refused to eat. This was a cause to worry immediately in the eyes of his parents, but Nuke had told them it was more of a personnel thing than a "nuclear" thing. "Don't worry about me." ,Nuke told them, "I'll be fine." However he was far from being "fine," as he was rather maladjusted in his frame of mind and outlook. Suddenly after all of these years, the "Sequoya" nuclear power plant became a battle ground for this young gentle man who handled the most unprocessed waste more than any of his fellow authorized employees there. As said, most of these plant's leading officials thought of people here like Nuke as less than important as they handle the waste, when in fact, they are the bravest and are the most likely to fall prey to this terrifying line of work. Besides, they keep the power plant a safe place, as these literally "unsung heroes" are the ones who institutions like these silently depend on.

It was early in the afternoon like any other day at the "Sequoya" nuclear plant in Tennessee, and Nuke was here at work, but was tense just the same in the midst of his private life. Today was the day when three gigantic transport truck-like vehicles arrived at the plant to receive the tons of raw and unprocessed nuclear waste that was in liquid form. Nuke was dressed in his white lead lined suit, with goggles, a special gas mask used in the field for this application, heavy black gloves that went to his elbows, and the dame for his feet, but went to the knees, and he wore a heavy duty Geigurcounter as he monitored the area before he performed any removal tactics as he had to check if the area was low in nuclear radiation. All was pretty quiet here as this was the norm concerning the area of the plant, which again only specially trained personnel could travel beyond this point as warnings are posted all over. Nuke went into the waste repository room No 1 and with a fellow employee who packed the waste into eight gallon drums specially designed to temporarily encapsulate before being processed or recycled, was hard at work in placing a special type of adhesive on the internal surface of the tops of each one of these barrels. Nuke went slowly back and forth at least fifty or more times when something disastrous happened, and would change the life of this kind young man forever.

Nuke was thinking to himself about how happy he was while being allowed to continue working here, when his colleague who liked Nuke very much, but never really bothered with the quiet man emotionally. They were doing what they are assigned to do as mentioned, and Nuke received a large barrel of the unprocessed liquid nuclear waste as it was placed carefully onto the heavy duty hand truck that Nuke held very carefully. He turned around and left the gigantic room which contained the plant's waste underground inside of storage tanks, which are accessed under the floor where his mentioned colleague was remaining and carefully filling the barrels. Nuke was completely silent while completing this vital and highly dangerous task as every part of his mind and body must be completely focused and crystal clear. Again, all was quiet and Nuke walked through the large area with a smooth concrete floor that has not been inspected in a while, when suddenly something snagged the left wheel of the hand truck that Nuke was pushing.

Nuke's senses were jarred into complete wakefulness when he felt himself suddenly falling to the left! His eyes widened as he prayed which spanned a mere second, that he would make it out of this alive, whatever it was that was now going on. He fell very quickly as and hit his head against the concrete flooring, which immediately caused the young man to briefly lose consciousness, but he was awake just enough to cry out for help. He was completely alone, but unbeknown to him, a friend who was very close, was just suited up and carrying a geirurcounter, heard

Nuke's crying for assistance, as it sounded pained somehow. When his friend ran out into the area, he sighted Nuke as the barrel of liquid waste had burst itself open, and the waste had spilled out all around him, as well as underneath! Dropping the geigercounter, his good friend ran over to Nuke and literally dragged him out of the growing puddle of nuclear waste, but unbeknown to this assisting man, some of the lethal substance was seeping into his lead lined suit and was burning his face, neck, arms and parts of his legs, as well as one of his hands. Nuke was screaming, but he was barely conscious as said. He ran toward the wall mounted phone in red or yellow, which was used only as an emergency, and told them a spill of nuclear waste had occurred, and there was a victim, and to send help immediately.

Alarms went off all around the place and a heavy, heavy solid lead door closed up to cordon off this contaminated area. Specialized paramedics were called on the scene, but would take some time, as they were located some one-hundred and fifty or more miles away from the vicinity of the plant. In the meantime, they moved Nuke as far away from the spilt waste as they could, but because of the literally hundreds of R.E.M.'S of nuclear radiation, he could not leave this now restricted area as it was highly contaminated as the deadly radiation would disperse all though the plant. Firefighting foam was placed over the spilt waste so as not to cause any further contamination, but "hazmat," or hazardous materials cleanup was called to come here as quickly as possible.

Nuke's friend, Justin was also one who came to check the area for the amount of radiation that may be loitering about here, but now he acted as the only gateway between consciousness and a possible coma for Nuke. He had the top to his suit removed, because he was screaming so loudly, as he was being savagely burned from the spilt nuclear waste as it made immediate contact with his skin. Nuclear waste, especially in this state, and adding to the fact of it being unprocessed, and making it less radioactive, continues to burn right through flesh, and it doesn't stop until it is washed away, as it is capable of going right through bone and then out again as it still burns it's hideously savage path. However, Nuke was in excruciating agony as he was slowly but surely slipping into shock and was becoming cold and shivered amidst the tremendous heat caused from this "contact" radiation.

The entire plant was notified by alarms as well as security, but what really gave the leading officials a good "visual" was the cameras placed everywhere throughout the plant. Nuke was seeing nothing but green although his eyes were closed tightly, which was also an autonomous reaction to feeling the liquid nuclear waste on his face. Justin as well as two others fellow waste workers here, rushed to his aid. Nuke was, by now, falling into deep unconsciousness as the helicopter flew over the nuclear power plant and searched for a tangible place to land. The sound of the engines were deafening as the blast from the rotors, or the air being pushed downward, was incredible as these specially trained paramedics came out of the aircraft with a stretcher, and were wearing protective suits themselves as they were informed ahead of time of a nuclear waste spill had occurred at the "Sequoya" nuclear power plant.

Everyone was told to get to the decontamination area as fast as they could following this terrible accident. By now, Nuke was taken outside as he was carried in the arms of two good friends, as Justin was one of them. Again, his head covering to the lead lined suit was removed as he was not only suffocating, but the waste had seeped onto his face as it just missed his mouth. With the tremendously loud sound of the helicopter in the near background, Nuke was immediately placed onto the stretcher but not strapped down just yet, as they had to check his burns, because they had come form a spill of deadly nuclear materials that were highly radioactive. Geigurcounters were used and the measurements of radioactivity were going off the charts. Nuke cried out as a painful, but mutilated scream erupted from his mouth while lying there as these two highly capable men were ca ring for him. It was decided that things would be easier if he was taken into the helicopter, and that way the equipment would be a great assistance.

The overcast day was certainly benidictive of something utterly gruesome as Nuke was inside and immediately airlifted off of the property of the nuclear power plant. As the helicopter flew off, everyone here, who could, watched them fly off as they wondered if they would ever see their good friend again. Suddenly the whole power plant seemed empty and cold-just like what these places truly are. In the meantime, the medical team removed the heavy white lead lined suit from Nuke as carefully as they could. He was attached immediately to I.V.'s to keep him hydrated as well as to receive medications. He was given morphine which put a figurative "dent" into the terrific pain he felt. Surprisingly though this whole time, which appeared to take an eternity, Nuke managed to remain somewhat conscious, but he realized that he felt strange in his mind, but this was purely form a medical perspective, and not a psychiatric one. His left side, where he hit up against the concrete flooring of the restricted area while carrying the waste, was somewhat paralyzed as the result of falling, and he couldn't talk, especially where now he had been innervated. They were cleaning the radioactive waste off of his body with a specialized cleaner, which was used in "haz-mat" accidents, as these same paramedics were trained only in the care of the victims of hazardous material accidents, and "Nuke" Wilcox was certainly no exception to the rule.

They notified the special radiation victim care facility which was located some one-hundred and fifty or more miles away about a victim of a spill of radioactive nuclear waste, but as they briefly outlined his overall condition, the response team at the facility was in shock, because they have never come up against one who was seemingly "covered" with raw nuclear waste. They were readying themselves at the facility, but they thought, God only knows what they will be in for in a matter of time. What will he look like? Will he be alive, and for how much longer? What will become of Nuke now?

All he ever wanted to do since he was a mere child, was to work in this nuclear power plant, and now what will his parents say about all of this? But first, the facility must receive him before any of this can be officially sorted out. Unknowingly, these people, like the nuclear power plant, will be receiving a "child" rather than an adult, as he was as innocent as innocent can be.

Nuke was teetering back and forth between consciousness and eternal sleep, as this specific part of his brain had lacked the concern which had so highly revolved around living and dying. He was taken to the landing pad where the helicopter touched down, and a news recovery team had already intruded the scene where this kindly young man was now savagely fighting for his very life. Cameras brought in this terrifying news, but unknowingly "Nuke's" parents had not been watching the television that time of day, and his father had the day off.

The chief of the "Sequoya" nuclear power plant in Tennessee called the immediate family notifying them of what happened to they're son here. The mother, Cellia Wilcox, answered the phone and heard the professional, but caring voice of a man on the other end of the line telling her that Nuke had fallen on the floor while carrying a barrel of raw liquid nuclear waste, and as this occurred, the barrel opened and spilled the waste all over the place and covered the area, which well included the body of they're son. If the lead lined suit was not on his person, and closed in the correct manner, then what had leaked inside would have been a lot more, and his body would have literally burned to death and "liquefied" right there on the spot. Cellia, while holding the receiver of the wall mounted telephone, gestured frantically for her husband Jake to come and listen. "It's the power plant! Nuke has been in an accident! Jake; hurry!" ,Cellia cried out to her husband, but in a whisper-like fashion so she could still remain listening to the words of extreme importance which were now being told to her. Jake, a rather large and husky man, but a handsome looking character, ran over to where his wife was standing and partially covering the speaker with her older hand which signified a lifetime of hard work and struggle. Jake took hold of the receiver gently from the now shaking hand of his dear wife, he asked the official, or the President of the "Sequoya" nuclear power plant, what actually happened, and if he would be so kind to repeat his testimony of the so called "accident." Cellia clung desperately onto the brawny shoulder of her loving husband who has supported the likes of his only son, and never once condemned him for loving all things nuclear. A business man himself, Jake asked calmly, but his writhing emotions that were witheld could be easily felt, as well as mildly heard in his pressured speech. "What happened to my son? ;: what do you mean he's been in an accident?-What kind of an accident?"

The President, or leading official who ran the plant, explained the same terrifying situation to Jake, but Jake suddenly interrupted the man's flowing speech and demanded to know where he was taken. "Where did you take Nuke?!" The leading official of the entire plant replied softly, but once again professionally, "You're son was airlifted off to the nuclear victim facility-it's a specially designed hospital where people who are victims of nuclear accidents and exposure are promptly taken for care, and like the power plant, everyone and the building is equipped to handle massive exposures to radioactivity and radiation poisoning. It's located about one-hundred and fifty-three miles from here. I'll fax you the directions right now. But, Mr. Wilcox...I wouldn't be too optimistic about him living if I were you. (Lowering his voice)...you're son won't make it...I'm so sorry." Suddenly, Jake yelled at him before hanging up, "Oh, yeah-you don't know Nuke-do you? He has something in him that people like you will never know." Jake immediately hung up the now sweaty receiver and embraced his shaking wife as he explained what happened to Nuke. She screamed. "NOOOO! NUKE! NOOOO! Oh, my God!" He received the f ax of the directions to the nuclear victim care facility and they quickly packed a couple of bags and loaded up the car and drove off into the approaching night.

In the meantime, doctors and specially trained nursing personnel suited in lead lined apparel and carrying geigurcounters, monitored the amount of high levels of nuclear radiation which literally emulsed forth from his person that was so badly burned. He was stripped further and raced into the operating room, but the hazardous material paramedics were lucky enough to stabilize this dying young man. As they frantically raced Nuke into the operating room, the poor man was fighting the innervation tube as he tried to cry out from such agony as he was so badly burned form the nuclear waste almost covering his body, but especially his cheeks, and arms, anterior chest and the upper posterior back and the neck, as this was all because of the said waste leaking in from the natural openings in the suit, as these special garments of protective wear were made in a few separate pieces.

They talked to Nuke to try and calm him down, while an anesthetist injected his i.v. with a copious does of an anesthetic called "Propofol," which is made from egg whites. He was out in a moment. They x-rayed his thyroid, which is an organ that loves nuclear radiation as it absorbs very easily and is always checked on all employees who work at nuclear power plants, especially on the way out after each work day. Nuke's thyroid had to be removed immediately or he will die in a matter of hours, as well as a parathyroid had to succumb to the same fate. They removed some of his lymphatics under the arms, because they were already swollen five times they're size and would burst, hence spreading deadly poison all through his body. They checked the massive burns and wrapped them as burn specialists entered here as well, as a trach team had entered this place as they were called to remain on "stand-by" in case they were needed to save Nuke's life that was failing right before their eyes. He was typed and cross matched as he required a blood transfusion immediately as was also discovered that calcium was beginning to leave his cellular structures, which meant that Nuke would die in less that six hours, but they were not going to give up on this brave victim who was fighting upon arrival. Not to mention, all seemed to sense something emerging from this young man that appeared to touch them. To keep him from lapsing into shock, especially from the massive radiation burns, he was placed on a copious amount of fluid with electrolytes and antibiotics. His marrow was beginning to fail, and he was already banked from the blood bank, but shortly after he received this critical operative care, Nuke received a PICC line, which is a central intravenous cathider that is placed into a large vessel in the arm, preferably the tridial vessel, which is inside of the arm, and is tunneled through this point of entry which goes up into the superior vena cava of the heart where there is the most fluid in the body to receive the foods and can displace the contents, but not just foods, but fluids, medications, blood, as well as blood draws, and pretty much any kind of direct injection infusion.

After what appeared like an eternity, Nuke was taken into I.C.U. and was kept unconscious from drugs to keep him from lapsing into shock, but not too sedated as this would have a reverse effect and cause the man to die. He was isolated behind makeshift barriers in the specially designed I.C.U. as he was giving off literally hundreds of R.E.M.'s of deadly nuclear radiation, as this would happen for a total of six-to-seven weeks following. However in the meantime, Nuke would have to make it through the first twenty-four hours, which is the most critical time for any patient who endures a traumatic injury, and never mind a spill of nuclear waste that fell onto the victim. He was asleep and seemed to be at peace, but when his parents arrived some hours later, they were in for possibly the biggest shock of they're lives.

Chapter Four

CELLIA AND JAKE WILCOX arrived at the facility no later then 10:23 p.m. that night. They were first intercepted by doctors who asked them of they're identities, which was testified in a manner of starkness and petrifying disbelief over what happened, especially where the couple had not yet laid eyes on their son. The doctors calmly explained to them exactly what happened to Nuke from a medical perspective, as well as outlining what he had to endure that night upon arrival here. They were informed of the traumatic sight that will come upon them, but despite the warnings, the couple who loved they're son went to see him, but even then they could not go anywhere near the young man, but rather view him from a special lead glass petition so they could look inside of the room that now housed Nuke. The parents of Nuke held each other as they cried, but all was quiet here during this time of the night, as all other victims were either asleep or awake and facing uncontrollable medical agonies.

The worried parents saw Nuke lying on his back in the special hospital bed with an air mattress to take the weight off of his body that was so burned form not only radiation, but from the nuclear waste coming into contact with his skin. Nuke was unconscious and his cheeks were gently bandaged, while his neck was wrapped in burn cloths as well as his arms, while parts of his hands that were not affected, remained untouched and exposed to the air. He was innervated and his hair was falling away form his head in literal handfuls as it now covered all around the sides of the pillow, as most of it had already fallen away from the nuclear radiation, which as of now, his body still emitted hundreds of R.E.M.S, hence no one but trained medical personnel could enter this special room that now contained they're only son. He was receiving a transfusion of whole blood, which included the white blood cells, or what is known as "leucocytes," as they were desperately attempting to get his marrow back into working order as it suppressed and as mentioned before, calcium was leaving his cellular structures, which meant sure death for the young nuclear waste worker. As the couple looked at they're gentle son lying there completely unconscious as well as in equal proportion to helplessness, something traumatic went through the minds of this couple in pertinence to the nuclear power plant, as well as how it ignored Jake's personal investigation regarding the continuous low level of "safe" nuclear radiation he was being exposed to since he entered this place of his dreams.

They looked all about the outside of the room containing Nuke, and they saw these "wheels" all over the place, as well as on Nuke's Johnny, as they later found the garments these victims wore was only to differentiate them between nuclear victims and those who are not. But in the present meantime, Cellia and Jake Wilcox cried here together as they held each other to bring the other comfort in this trying and terrifying hour of need and premature grieving and loss. Just before they left to stay at the hotel for the night, a lead suited clad nurse entered the room with more medication to place into Nuke's intravenous cathider loitering in his arm, which the couple saw and had no inkling of it's purpose and meaning. Jake listened to the geigurcounter as it's sound sped up, which indicated extremely high levels of nuclear radiation in the contaminated area. They couldn't bare this any longer, so the parents, so filled with love for they're son, left the tragic scene.

While they quietly left here, they walked down the maze of halls and lead petitions, which again contained the "wheel" signifying anything radioactive or nuclear, they held each other's hand and looked from side to side as if trying some way to wrap themselves around what has happened, and how all of their lives have changed forever, because of a spill of nuclear waste. Cries of agony were heard as they passed by, while there was one patient, worse then Nuke, who was nothing but a living burn, and had been poisoned with nuclear isotopes. A nurse was assisting him as the loud sound of oxygen was heard all through this one room, as each patient was allowed private lodgings. There was another nuclear scientist who worked in a nuclear power plant like they're son, and he was an older man, but was actively dying as tonight was possibly his final night here upon the earth. He cried and cried as he was a victim of an accident similar to Nuke's, but rather than falling with spilling nuclear waste, he fell head first into the cooling pond, or pool where the massive proton rods are kept to cool, but this water is not just water, but boric acid is added to it to make them less radioactive. He screamed and sustained massive brain damage, but the pain was so bad, that he was already in a drug induced coma to keep the scientist comfortable until he died in only a matter of hours, which may lapse into no more than three days maximum. This place was like Hell on earth as it was filled with unconscionable agony of the body and the living soul as accidents happen in places as these nearly every day. Tears spewed from the eyes of Cellia as she desperately clung to the strong hand of her brawny, stocky husband while continuing they're trek through this terrible and sorrowful place of truly inconceivable suffering. They wonder to themselves, natural nuclear energy and power is one thing; God has created that specific form, but not the manner in which man has done over the last one-hundred years or so when he discovered how plutonium, and it's various forms, have been extracted and manipulated to destroy, as well as to create energy for peaceful purposes. As said, spills and all kinds of accidents happen everywhere across the world that people do not hear about, and now the parents of they're gentle and kind son, who simply loved working in a nuclear power plant, lies here in this same tragic facility where people come to die such horrific deaths, or if they leave here, their lives are surely never the same. The worried parents wondered to themselves in a series of completely separate thoughts, Will Nuke survive?-and if he does-will he be all right enough to live a fairly normal life again?

At this point in time they knew there was nothing further they could do to help Nuke, but the loving parents prayed endlessly for him to just wake up and hear them. Pain and unimaginable grief struck them like a speeding train as they cried during the whole two days they remained there on the outside of his lead petitioned room. Exhaustion set in, so the Wilcox's left for home, which was only about four miles away from the "Sequoya" nuclear power plant where Nuke has worked since he was twenty. However through al of this, the "Department of Energy" was immediately sent to this power plant the following day while the Wilcox's were not present as they kept prayer vigil. This accident, according to the news media circuit, apparently shook the nation apart, because of it's apparent "stupidity." These assigned officials from the Department checked out not only the highly radioactive scene that was cordoned off where the spill had actually taken place, but the eight gallon barrel had been confiscated as evidence, but before it was removed for further investigation, photographs were taken of the barrel, the floor, as well as the "Haz-Mat" team who was now in the arduous process of cleaning up the mass of spilt radioactive waste. In the meantime, the "Department of Energy" personally visited the home of the parents of "Nuke" Wilcox, who is the poor victim now clinging to life at the nuclear victim care facility. The representatives from the "Department of Energy" spoke professionally and candidly with the severely distraught couple who apparently loved they're son very, very much, but while the Wilcox's spoke to them, they often cried such overwhelming emotions as they explained to the exactly what had been told to them by the power plant officials during the very day of this terrible accident, as well as what they actually saw that night several hours after "Nuke" was mended and resting comfortably, but was still very much in severe critical condition. However there existed one powerful statement which Cellia Wilcox, the mother of Nuke, told the Department and the news, which was this," When my husband and I arrived to see "Nuke" that night of the accident, we couldn't be anywhere near him, because he was so radioactive, and we would have gotten radiation sickness like our son has right now. Instead, Jake and I had to stand behind lead glass petitions with a ventilation system inside of the room so we could see him and be with him—We wouldn't even hold one of his badly burnt hands as a very possible "good-bye." Cellia Wilcox cried bitterly in the arms of Jake.

As said, Cellia cried as she was expressing her very starkly told statement that suddenly evolved into the beginning of a testament of they're son's horrific tragedy that never should have happened as it eventually shook the American nation, as well as the "National Department of Energy."

The department inspected the "Sequoya" power plant for several weeks as well as checked files, which were found loitering in hiding of "Nuke" Wilcox's daily regimen of low level nuclear radiation, which they immediately cited these leading officials. What was mostly striking to the "Department of Energy," was all of the secrecy when anything pertained to "Nuke" Wilcox, as even his past medical records which were confiscated, revealed that Nuke was examined thoroughly from their physicians, and a bogus report was written as well as an illegal "profile," which meant they were criticizing the young man about being too "possessive" of working with the nuclear waste, and it was seen on cameras which are located throughout this place, that he was seemingly "taking refuge" in places that are "contaminated" with radiation. Of course, this was absolutely bogus, as Nuke knew nothing about this, as well as most of the leading officials. However what had been very quickly discovered in pertinence to the barrel, was that the special adhesive that gets stronger with time, was not placed around the inside of the opening in a copious enough fashion, which spelled out catastrophe and appalling disaster for Nuke, as well as the entire power plant. The cement flooring that is located here in this special area of the plant where Nuke transferred the barrels of waste, one at a time, carefully and very responsibly, but now the Department inspected not only the photos taken, but later they did the same with the actual floor, which had many other cracks in it, but luckily none of these were anywhere near the path Nuke had taken to transfer the raw nuclear waste. In the meantime, they could not inspect the actual area right away, but rather had to wait, due to the radiation being so high, as this same area of the plant had been immediately shut down and sealed off.

Nuke was resting comfortably for quite a while, but he was moved to his own room in five days after he arrived here at the nuclear radiation victim care facility. Again, he was in his own room as there was a microphone in the room so the patient could speak to his/her visitors who may be loitering on the other side. Nuke was stabilizing miraculously well, and two weeks later he attempted to moan, as the enervation tube was removed some time ago as he was now breathing on his own. Nuke's voice was barely heard, but he let out a very prolonged groan, "AAAAAAAAHHHHHHHHHHH." The nursing staff heard Nuke's voice, and they raced to his room here at the facility, and. still giving off copious amounts of nuclear radiation, the poor young man lies here helpless and spoke to the two medical professionals who entered his room. In a choked, but very raspy voice, Nuke said in broken speech to them clad in white lead lined suits, "AAAAAAHHHHHHHH…. Power plant….power plant. I spilt nuclear waste…all over me. Help me…help me…." They comforted him and assured Nuke that everything was all right and that they knew all about what had happened to him. He drooled and rolled his eyes in back of his head, but moved them back in their direction once more. He looked so incredibly helpless as well as "gentle" as Nuke was a poor innocent victim of a spill at the nuclear power plant, which was the same plant he loved and dreamed of working in since early boyhood. They went to get the correct physicians to check on Nuke and see if he is all right as to be expected in this terrible condition he is now in, especially where his apparent survival is nothing short of miraculous.

The nurses who are highly specialized in this specific area of medicine approached the situation very carefully, especially where this man is concerned. The team of two physicians who have been caring for "Nuke" since his emergency arrival into this shielded hospital room, also wearing protective lead lined suits to keep them safe from the staggering amount of nuclear radiation that appeared to engulf this poor victim's body. Upon entering the room where Nuke was kept, his mouth widened more to one side when he turned his head to face these caring professionals as they now arrived. Nuke's voice was very mutilated at first, especially where he had just awakened from the heavy stupor that was the byproduct of drugs and from the terrible trauma his body had thusly sustained. He eyed them without words, although he remained calmed, but in a terrible amount of agony from the burns as well as the radiation itself, but Nuke quickly answered them when questions were asked. Yet upon answering them, the physicians checked his vital signs and other things regarding necessity, Nuke appeared like his old self, especially where his memory had not at all been affected from this blunt trauma when he fell onto the cement floor back at the plant. However his voice was gentle as it had always been, but because Nuke could not motion his mouth very well now, the man appeared to have sustained considerable brain damage as a result from the excessive amount of nuclear radiation that bombarded his body and despite the fact that he was properly shielded with his lead lined suit. However the faulty design that included all suits in this way, save for the type used in bio laboratories, which are all constructed of one exclusive covering, had caused some of the thick and highly viscous radioactive nuclear waste to seep into the inner part of the lead suit, hence as to why this man's body had become so badly burned as four layers of the seven layer construction of the skin had literally been "melted' away. In fact, If the highly specialized paramedics had not known how to wash away this deadly nuclear waste from his skin, Nuke's arms would have been amputated, because the waste, which was unprocessed and not neutralized, would only have continued to burn until there was nothing left for it to consume.

Nuke answered their questions easily in his mutilated voice like, "Do you know where you are?" and "What happened to you?" Nuke's personality was somewhat the very same, except he was most definitely confused, because of his whereabouts. However this was all explained to him, which this information just provided had not eluded Nuke's understanding sense. Too weak to be subjected to certain medical tests they wanted to perform right now, but an E.E.G. was done to check and see just how much of Nuke's brain had been damaged from this terrible nuclear accident. Nuke only rolled his eyes around the rather small room and slowly verbally communicated with the caring and ethical medical staff. The poor man learned he was placed into a specialized medical facility for victims of nuclear accidents, but this said information at present, had not at all appeared to matter to the man in any negative manner. However Nuke asked them why they were all wearing lead lined suits and holding onto geigercounters like he had while working at the 'Sequoya" nuclear power plant as this made him suddenly miss his friends there, as well as the sense of self in which Nuke had endlessly worked so hard to achieve.

It had been calmly explained to "Nuke" that his body had absorbed at least 500 R.E.M.'S of nuclear radiation, hence the reason for their apparel. Nuke only rolled his bald head from one side and laughed in a very feeble way that was reactive to their words of otherwise terrifying tragedy, and said to them, "Ah, ha...I'm radioactive. That's funny... Ha, ha...I'm radioactive....radioactive." His smile was twisted and opened like in the same manner as a mentally retarded person might respond, but it was more as if he was a child who was devoid of realistic comprehension, which these professionals took immediate notice of his overall reaction to what was said. However, Nuke was not like this at all. He was terribly aware and clear headed, but his understanding would only grow less cloudy the more his mind awakened from this tragedy. But rather, the man was merely trying to accept just what had occurred.

Nuke's emaciated body was already atrophying and he discovered his hair was gone completely from the scalp, but very surprisingly, this terrifying tragedy that had suddenly fallen into this man's lap had not at all bothered him with much ferocity as all suspected would, but how wrong they were. Nuke wanted to know if he could see his parents so they were notified later on that same day of his official awakening. The immense shock this couple sustained as they listened over the telephone so intently as they heard they're son was now awake, somewhat alert, as well as coherent, as well as the fact that Nuke was asking for his parents was all significant of a very plausible miracle. The couple cried in relief of they're vigilant prayers coming true, but the senior physician caring compassionately for "Nuke" informed them a little about what he looks like, and the fact that they're had suffered a very considerable amount of brain damage, but it was very difficult to differentiate as to just how much of the said brain damage was from the concussion, or from the massive amount of nuclear radioactivity his body had absorbed.

Either way one looks at it, this man suffered a great deal and was agony, as there already had been numerous vital procedures and operations he underwent in order to save his life, or at least what remains of it.

Again the parents of this young victim felt profoundly angered at the power plant for merely allowing an accident as this to happen, and especially where this place of work was always so safe as well as perfectly abiding in all areas of the mentioned issue concerning safety, and where no life of an employee should ever be compromised. The Wilcox's immediately went to the nuclear care facility to visit they're son, but once more the couple could only view him from behind shields of heavy lead glass, but this time, a conversation could be carried out. Tears of a tremendous grief ran from Cellia's eyes, and on occasion, from those of Jake, her husband-the parents of "Nuke"-as they diligently tried to speak with him in this way that seemed so impersonal. However in the midst of speaking to him, it had been seen immediately by Cellia, that "there was something wrong with him." Meaning, he opened his mouth while turning his head to the side to face them as they stood there behind the lead glass of this facility used to care for and to house patients of nuclear accidents or radiation poisoning. He, "Nuke," only moaned at them, but the man spoke to them nonetheless, yet his manner of speaking was rather varied in it's tone and flow. The poor man sounded as if he had awakened form a coma or from a major operation, yet no sadness appeared to go forth into the outer realm of the senses. Worry literally plagued the loving parents, especially now that they had seen him just a day after awakening from his unconscious catatonic state. The man was in a sea of literal agony from the burns which had been caused by the raw and unprocessed nuclear waste making contact with his body beneath the suit. With glassy eyes that were surrounded with excessively exaggerated eye sockets, the young man only stared groggily at them, but Nuke had undoubtedly recognized them and just who they were; these two loving people standing on the other side of the glass and who still could not go near him or touch him, because he was simply too radioactive.

It was strikingly clear to them, and because of the team of specialists, Nuke had sustained severe injury to his systems from the exposure to a very copious amount of nuclear radiation. Even today, with all of the major advances in understanding and caring for various medical conditions, it is still very much uncertain to many as to just how overdoses of nuclear radiation, or even "background radiation" reacts with the body's tissues, it's cellular structures, or organelles. However what is known is the body, although highly resilliant, can very easily break down at an alarming rate whenever exposed to this amount of radiation and nuclear chemicals and materials, whether they are naturally or artificially produced. It is clearly known that radioactive materials emit penetrating ionizing radiation which can very easily injure living tissues and other organisms. An exposure to 500 R.E.M.'S is always lethal, but with great surprise, "Nuke" somehow managed to live—but for how long?

Chapter Five

CONVERSATIONS WERE COPIOUSLY CARRIED out by the parents of this gentle young man who fell victim to such a horrible disaster that could have easily been avoided, but still no one had come forward to rectify what happened. Jake and Cellia Wilcox, the loving parents of Nuke, had done the best they could in retaining they're truest emotions concerning this horrible situation which may mean the end of they're son's life. He was diagnosed with radiation sickness, but his condition was more likened to when someone survives a nuclear bomb explosion, or when a nuclear power plant explodes like in 1979 at Three Mile Island. It was truly an impossibility to actually have Nuke still alive in this deplorable state, but for some reason which is otherwise completely unknown to anyone, they're son was more than alive, but coherent, but certainly not without damage.

The parents of Nuke heard horror stories from experts here at the facility telling them that Nuke will end up dying a horrible death very soon, and he will cease breathing, or he will only lapse into shock before falling into a deep coma, and then to only die. All of this otherwise truthful medical information told to them would have happened, but so far had not. There obviously was a reason why they're son had lived, but so far the said reason was yet to be known. Nuke was crying in a silent form of untold agony whenever his burn cloths were changed, or when he should receive treatments to help his body metabolize the nuclear radiation that was being harbored within his body's tissues and systems, and never mind when he would be washed while there in bed. The total parenternal nutrition, which was fed to Nuke through his PICC line that had been implanted into his left arm when he first arrived, as well as received most of his medications through this as well, and his fluids and antibiotics. Nuke threw up every time something went into his rapidly shriveling stomach that was practically nonexistent. He was also catheterized as Nuke could no longer rise from his hospital bed in any way, especially because of the fact that he was so profoundly weakened from his body attempting to combat the radiation's invasional attack against all of his body's various and elaborate systems. However in the present meantime, he was receiving excellent medical and spiritual care, which everyone in this family was profoundly pleased to see and to know. Nuke, so far, felt no malice against anyone, although he could very easily recall vividly everything that happened the day when he had fallen with the barrel of raw nuclear waste. In midst of Nuke's speaking in a feeble manner, his overall message was somewhat clear to all who heard, and that was this; "It was no one's fault, but mine."

What seemed to worry both the parents of Nuke as well as the string of specially trained doctors, was that the man was not angered at anything, let alone his appalling medical condition, which much included his literal torturous agony in which he experienced on a daily basis from the burns as well as from deep inside of his bones. Still highly radioactive, Nuke often fell into peaceful stupors and smiled involuntarily, but this was done either when by himself, or when others were with him. It was discovered that Nuke had undoubtedly sustained a great deal of brain damage, but with the passing of time here, about three weeks since the terrible accident at the 'Sequoya" power plant, his manner of speaking became less and less withheld, but more open and freely thrashed about, especially with those who cared for him around the clock, as this is the kind of care Nuke will require for the rest of his life.

Nuke Wilcox seemed to melt into a world of reverting back to his childlike mannerisms, but then again Nuke always was this way when it should concern his personality. However since the accident, Nuke appeared to revel in his newfound helplessness and received the comfort he unconsciously craved veraciously. He seemed to feel completely devoid of worries whenever he should talk about the plant, his friends at the same power plant, as well as anything nuclear, which was a lot like when he was just a kid. Nuke was examined frequently, and his cheeks were badly burned, but after a time the rounded bandages were removed permanently, which revealed blackened skin, but his cheeks were really sunken in from his unholy ordeal. Nuke's thin arms still had special burn cloths on them, but when removed, silver was placed onto the badly burned skin, as it kills any lethal bacteria that enjoys to grow on burned bodies, especially where the epidermal layer is gone completely, and the muscle is thusly exposed, hence there are no nerve endings that tell the patient if there is heat or coolness. They gentle rolled almost transparent white cloths around and around his rapidly thinning arms in a spiral with the silver cream underneath. He, Nuke, merely lay here and allowed these loving professionals care for him, as the whole experience was a pleasure to all of this poor man's senses. A gentle, but wide, twisted smile emerged often as they would do this necessity to care for his savage burns made from the nuclear waste sitting on his skin. Sometimes, Nuke would laugh gently and his mouth would open itself wide involuntarily from the damage he has thusly endured. This place of death and horrific sorrow, and where most of these victims come to die, had undoubtedly become a place of happiness and life for one poor damaged individual, who was also the victim of a nuclear accident. Although his sense of awareness and connubiality had improved with each passing week here, it was abundantly clear that Nuke Wilcox was severely brain damaged from the excessive overdose of nuclear radiation, but unknowing to Nuke, his parents were talking with the "Department of Energy" about they're son. The "Sequoya" nuclear plant had a lot of explaining to do, as this was also the Department's sentiment as well concerning this individual. There was abundant evidence that proves this plant was completely and solely responsible for what happened to they're only son who is gentle and innocent as the child he had suddenly become, as the result of being so badly damaged from his accident, but Nuke was equally a man; an adult who could talk very rationally about all that has happened at the power plant and before that. The Department also went over the files, both bogus as well as those that are real. Something was definitely "fishy," and whatever it was could be smelled a long way away from the office. (The office of the Tennessee "Department of Energy.)

Yes, the "Department of Energy" had literally gone to the home of the Wilcox's and discussed things, but what was clearly certain, besides what had been discovered at the "Sequoya" power plant, was that the entire statewide chapter of the Department wanted to defend this victim and his family and to get them the compensation that is rightfully deserved.

During the many long and detailed synopses of what happened from all points of view, it was the victim's parents who expressed the most embittering forms of anger and profound sadness over the pathetic sights they have so far seen whenever visiting they're son at the special facility that cares for and harbors victims like Nuke. They were interview extensively while in the relative safety of they're home, which was only about four miles away from the "Sequoya" nuclear power plant. Cellia, the mother of Nuke, expressed avidly her angst as well as her profound grief over all that has so far happened, as well as the fact of her finding out that he has suffered extensive radiation sickness that will never be cured, as is the customary criteria, but in very rare cases some people have recovered successfully, but their lives have been permanently altered. There was a lot at stake here, and surprisingly, the representatives from the "Department of Energy" wanted them to have restitution as badly as they did. What had been explained to the couple, was that over a lapse of considerable time, professionals from the Department here in Tennessee have already extensively inspected not only the barrel that held the unprocessed nuclear waste that was still very highly radioactive, but there was an added reason for them to project more worry in the eyes of this couple.

Meaning, most nuclear power plants process, at least partially, their nuclear waste that comes from transfer tanks, the waste repositories, which are localized in very large rooms and kept underground, but after a time, the waste is carefully manipulated by robot, because of such high levels of radiation. From here, the waste is subjected to a very hot molten glass that is specially formulated to encapsulate it and make the waste more safe, which is called "brick." The brick is pumped into the special barrel through metal tubes, and again done by robots on site, and after this process is completed, the top of the container is welded closed in a manner of seven seconds, which is a lot of power in one small space, hence there is very little room for human error, but unfortunately this was not the way it happened that particular day when they're son handled the waste. Again, this brick glass that looks like white sand and literally makes the high level radioactive waste less radioactive, or what is known as "low rad" waste. The two representatives from the Department helped this couple acquire special lawyers who deal in this kind of situation, and especially where the evidence and the information that had been recently told to them, this was now a criminal investigation.

The folders or files which held personal information on Nuke Wilcox, as said, were not good, as there were many accusations against his character, which according to the Department, did not make sense. He was not a criminal, nor made any inkling that he may be a nuclear terrorist, as was suspect some months ago, but again representatives here knew that bogus files were planted, which luckily had been found and by the correct people. However it had been asked to this couple, the parents of Nuke, if they're son seemed to return from work preoccupied, or complaining of illness. They were obviously careful not to say too much, but what was clear to these representatives, was that Nuke Wilcox was, for some reason that was completely unknown to anyone, except to the accusers, had been seen clearly on motion camera at the plant, and had written that "he liked to hide out somewhere by himself, but especially where he may very easily risk his life by means of purposeful exposure to lethal nuclear radiation." It had been seen and recorded many times as this was a complete shock to the parents of the victim. However despite all of this supposed accusations allegations and conjecturing, it was most definitely believed by the Department that Nuke Wilcox had not been responsible for what had just happened to him at the plant. Overwhelming evidence pointed to negligence by those that closed these containers, as well as allowing him to transfer this waste to transport completely unsupervised and alone. "This is highly illegal." ,explained the "Department of Energy."

The parents of Nuke were infuriated and nothing short of it, after hearing what had been said about they're son who was perfectly innocent, as the Department already well knew and understood. This newly discovered information that had been told to them about Nuke, shattered they're conceptions, but not of they're son, but rather that of the individuals who ran the nuclear power plant. Jake, was who was a foundry worker in his late fifties, also a machinist, was well knowing about certain things pertaining to this power plant here in their community, but until he was spoken to by two reps from the "Department of Energy," the man felt stupid regarding his belief in the system. They both were left in shock and filled with more questions than they started with. What really angered them mostly, were the files that were shown, as these were proved right away as bogus by the Department, which it was highly suspect that "Nuke" was a nuclear terrorist who played "dumb" until he found the right opportunity to take over the plant. However he was never brought in for questioning, or removed from the plant by anyone, least of all the F. B. I. It was clearly seen by his parents that Nuke was being used as a scapegoat for some completely unknown reason. They had thought it was perhaps, that Nuke was so quiet and a gentle personality, that was a cause of suspicion with the leading plant officials. Either way, they knew the "Department of Energy" was going to eventually visit Nuke at the facility, and if he hears what was suspected of him, the young man may fall into a traumatic psychological state that just might cause his demise earlier.

The Department waited until it was safe for them to physically enter Nuke's room to talk to him about his experience at the power plant which led him here and to a premature death. It had taken a total of seven weeks for Nuke's body to metabolize the nuclear radiation, hence he was no longer considered as "radioactive." They introduced themselves as representatives from the "Department of Energy." Nuke was happy and more coherent than ever before, but he still had a ways to go. He shook they're hands gently, but also made an attempt to do this kindly act in the manner he used to before the accident that robbed him of much brain function. The representatives were the same individuals who had already spoken with his parents at the house some one-hundred and fifty or so miles away so there would not be any confusion regarding gathering information from both parties. Nuke was lying in his hospital bed and he was now receiving his parenternal nutrition as it was done here around the clock where he could not eat as a tumor had grown in his stomach in which nothing could pass, while the other port in the PICC line was pumping normal saline to hydrate him. Nuke was serious, but child-like when he explained what happened to him. They listened very intently and emphatically while they recorded all that he had said to them in a log. Nuke seemed very tired, in great physical pain, but not too much in any mental distress, which to them, was hard to fathom in a situation like this that destroys life rather than to save it. However it was most definitely clear to these two representatives that he remembered everything that happened, but he repeatedly blamed no one; not even the plant.

Nukes words: "I carried the nuclear waste…to…to…the transport truck at the back of the plant…..I wore my white lead suit like I always do…ahh…I guess I lost my balance or somethin' and I fell to my left?... And, I hit my head HARD on the floor, but no one was there…later my friend came as I saw him in his suit like mine…he had geeigercounter in his hand like I usually do, and ahh…..ahh…I felt burning and I saw inside the suit-nuclear waste coming in! NUCLEAR WASTE. I saw green the whole time I was asleep and when I kinda woke up in the airlift on the way here, then my suit was off and I was being washed with a chemical to get off the waste from me. Uh, uh…It wasn't the plant's fault-it was no one's fault-I fell in the nuclear waste. Now I'm radioactive…Ha ha ha." (Nuke smiles both voluntarily and involuntarily as he pulls up the heavy covers of his bed over his bare forearms. His terribly gaunt face was well benidictive of a suffering soul who had obviously well recalled the incident, but he was still lacking in some attributes necessary to achieve what he wanted to say to these caring gentlemen now before him. Nuke explained to them that he loved the nuclear power plant, and that this had been his lifelong dream to work there, or in some other nuclear facility. He studied hard since he was a child, as his father bought him real college books on this subject since Nuke turned the age of twelve. They had seen that Nuke's I.Q. was labeled as superior, but there existed no tangible number to say just how much. However when Nuke had been told gently by these representatives from the Department, that the leading officials suspected him to be a nuclear terrorist. Nuke laughed like a child who heard a funny joke, as it was well evident to them by his very realistic reaction that these accusations made by the plant, that he took what they had to say with a "grain of salt." Nuke said while laughing gently and his mouth wide open, "Me-a nuclear terrorist? Ha, Ha, Ha! They're funny over at the plant. It was probably my friends kidding around with the officials...I'm no terrorist, ha, ha, I love that power plant. Ha Ha Ha." They could see that he was completely innocent in every way, and it was truly a travesty in the manner in which officials at the power plant have handled this, especially concerning this victim now lying there before them.

Amidst this prolonged conversment, Nuke wavered back and forth in a consistent manner between wanting to get up and go back to work at the power plant he loves and claims to sensate no malice towards, to that of his innocent demeanor which won him this notorious notoriety as someone not completely certain of just where he stood in life and in society, but these feelings he possessed all these years, have been experienced from so deeply within that Nuke hadn't the slightest inkling of their existence. However as Nuke talked calmly with these two caring professionals from the "Department of Energy," he felt stirrings of an intense comfort rather than something that was reflective of a threat, which was the one thing Nuke Wilcox had unknowingly been the victim of while working all of these years at the power plant. Nuke's voice was obviously characteristic of someone who had experienced severe brain damage from the radiation sickness he now has succumbed to and is dying from. He moved his limbs in a very jerky manner as the poor young man gestured them closer while speaking to them about what happened that infamous day when he fell into an open canister or barrel or raw and unprocessed liquid nuclear waste. His face was painfully thin and the cheeks, which were as gaunt as they were burnt, told a silent story to these representatives who now sat here before the young man who contained a memory, despite what happened, that was seemingly flawless. Tacit messages were given out by the Department as well, but these said messages were of sorrow and pity that was most definitely manifested amidst they're speaking to this badly damaged man. However Nuke seemed to be very calm and collected amidst all of this, especially after hearing form them about the bogus file entries and narratives written about him by leading plant officials, like vaguely saying that he was a nuclear terrorist, because of the manner in which

Nuke likes to merely hang around by himself during times when there was no work. It was probably a blessing that he couldn't really take this kind of information inward and feels the full emotional thrashing these officials meant to do to this kind and innocent individual. Nuke told these officials from the "Department of Energy" flat out, but done in a rather gentle mode of speaking, "I guess they don't like me, because I'm quiet and I like to…to keep by my…self. I have a lot of good friends at the nuclear power plant." By now, it was redundantly clear to these two representatives that the young man was a victim of much more than a life altering accident.

The parents of Nuke were interviewed about three months following this terrible accident at the "Sequoya" power plant. It was done at the house of this loving couple who loved they're son more than anything in the world and it was obvious in an utmost painful manner that what happened at the power plant affected these people in a very traumatic way. Jake and Cellia Wilcox, the parents of Nuke, share some of they're truest feelings in pertinence to not only what happened there, but also how the officials at this once trusted power plant are so far handling this appalling and unspeakable tragedy that the "Department of Energy" is persistently saying to all who will listen, "There is no excuse or reason for such gross neglect of protocol."

MOTHER, Cellia Wilcox: "I will never forget when we received the call rom the plant where our son worked. (sigh)…My husband was not working that day, thank God, and I gestured for him to come to the telephone…and…we both listened to what the chief of the "Sequoya" power plant had to tell us. "Nuke" was in an accident and now fighting for his life…There is just no way I can even begin to imagine what really happened to him."

FATHER, Jake Wilcox:: "No, I too couldn't believe it. He had been working steadily at this power plant since he was twenty; just got out of college as he worked and studied fro three years straight, and with barely any vacation. It's all he ever wanted to do-to work at a nuclear power plant. According to the officials, he didn't have quite enough necessary education to assist him in any form of higher level of work there, but he was a good waste handler, they said, hence Nuke had been doing this same job for twenty-one years."

MOTHER, Cellia Wilcox: "Nuke" has always been a good person. He loves anything nuclear, but he loves peace at the same time. I still have trouble believing that the "Sequoya" nuclear power plant is trying to cover up what really went concerning our son. We have been visiting him almost every few days, and although the traveling distance is far from where we live, it doesn't at all matter to us. What really matters to us is the health of "Nuke," and things have changed for him considerably as well as catastrophically. We didn't know he was even going to live and never mind become coherent like he is now, although we have trouble understanding him most of the time as he smiles at us involuntarily."

FATHER, Jake Wilcox: "According to the plant officials, everyone was doing their jobs as they should, but just what would be the cause of someone falling and then having a barrel of nuclear waste OPEN and spill all over you? I'll tell you, in my personal opinion, that's bullshit. They know exactly what happened, and we as his parents are not going to stop fighting them until they start telling the truth and fess up to their fatal mistake, as well as these horrific bodily injuries that have changed the very life of our son forever. The radiation sickness he now has as the result of this terrible accident will no doubt, end his life prematurely. As his parents, we've always known our son to be someone who doesn't, in any way, attempt to rattle cages or cause trouble, or to make the lives of others miserable, but rather he does just the opposite. 'Nuke" gives freely of himself every day, and all done in a gentle manner that is often unbecoming of a man, but he's more of a man than most I have seen, especially concerning this situation that out son was a victim of.

The "Department of Energy' assisted them on a very personal level as they not only immediately went on site to investigate this rather appalling situation that should never have happened, but as said, they went to the home of the parents of "Nuke" and spoke to them about in assisting them in any manner they could. The lawyers who represented the couple who had been found by the Department, were struck with an almost surreal form of shock as they were interviewed by the Department officials who have been so far handling this rather perplexing case that appeared to be harboring some kind of cover up in regards to the feelings that were, at least right now, reserved by those at the power plant. These attorneys had also looked over the same pictorial evidence that was provided to them by the "Department of Energy," and they found the same infutible evidence that the officials from the Department had equally found, especially when concerning the barrel or the container used to temporarily encapsulate the raw nuclear waste, as this also included the flooring where they're son walked that particular day, which is a day that will live in a cold and bitter infamy for both the parents, and possibly they're dying son who before that said day was healthy, or so it appeared.

'Nuke" gladly told his story to the small band of lawyers who finally met him at the special nuclear victim care facility as he was still very obviously fighting for his very life, but done in a manner that eluded fear for the young and innocent man who was childlike in every way and as he always had been. These specially trained individuals, along with crucial file evidence provided by his string of specialty physicians and experts in this field of medicine, it was equally seen and decided by all prosecuting parties, that this was an inexcusable accident that was most likely caused from sheer negligence. In court, the "Department of Energy" defended the couple, or the parents of the victim, as photographic evidence was certainly well depicted and allowed in this lengthy case that was sent into a rather quick resolve. But despite the consistent showing of the barrel and the floor, the officials from the "Sequoya" nuclear power plant still very openly refused to take responsibility for their completely negligent actions which are completely inexcusable in a profession as this. Again despite this overwhelming evidence that had most definitely proven this was the fault of the plant, the overall situation was most definitely heard and taken very seriously by everyone here, the ever encroaching media; except by those at the plant. The leading officials of the "Sequoya" power plant were not present to comment on this pressing situation as they out right refused all communications from the media as well as from lawyers which were given to the Wilcox family, the family of the victim, exclusively by the help of the Department.

The young man known to all as "Nuke," had been somewhat kept unconcerned by the radiation sickness which he now suffers a great deal from as the product of such negligence. He was visited often by friends from the power plant who truly cared a great deal for Nuke and his welfare. Some could not see Nuke again, because the sight of him was too much of an ordeal to emotionally bear, while others came to see him again and again. One person in particular, his name was Greg Thompson, who was a nuclear safety engineer, and forged a relative close bond with the young man who handled the plant's nuclear waste for twenty-one years. They have always called each other silly names like "shithead," "dumb ass," and "dink weed." Upon entering Nuke's room here at the facility, each of them would not say a word at first, but would rather give out the "finger" and smile as they used to do at the plant. In fact, the plant received a whole new shipment of danger signs with the "nuclear wheel," as what Nuke has always called this three pronged symbol for anything nuclear or radioactive. He decorated Nuke's room, all over it's walls, with signs as these from the plant so Nuke wouldn't feel so sad and homesick for not only his place of work, which was the only type of work he knew, but also reminiscent of the area of the state where he once lived. The specially trained psychiatrists worried about this, but surprisingly, these signs never at all bothered Nuke, because it reminded him of just what his friend anticipated; also his bedroom back home, which he also greatly missed, but does not mention to anyone as he keeps things as this to himself. In a matter of sorts, Nuke's room here was all things nuclear like back home, which he truly enjoyed as he said to some trusting people in his now completely altered life, "It takes some of the sting out of being far away from home, and from the power plant; from my friends."

Chapter Six

THIS WHOLE LEGAL BATTLE proved extremely tough on the Wilcox's, especially where they didn't want to reveal anything to they're suffering son until everything was over and a settlement or conclusion was established to suit both parties. It was very hard during the long court sessions, because of the leading plant officials literally showing no level of concern for they're son's horrific suffering and the fact that he is now losing his life to radiation sickness, and never mind the extensive burns, the removal of his thyroid, and a tumor in his stomach, which surgeons now suggest a gastrotomy, or to the lay person, total removal of the stomach organ, and that he must receive all of his nutrients and fluids through an intravenous line implanted into his arm for the rest of his life, which regarding as to how much time Nuke has remaining. No one yet knows, especially where the poor man should have died that day. The medical files spoke candidly of absolute terrifying horror, which had even caused some of the plant officials to visibly quake and revert to quietness. What was so unbelievable, was the leading plant officials snubbed the Wilcox's amidst they're traumatic psychological agony over the condition of thcy'rc son.

Nuke was most certainly never going to get better; he was dying and there is certainly no cure for severe radiation sickness, but in the midst of the tremendous scrutiny about the poor man's acquired medical condition that is really disguised as a terminal illness, Nuke remained the peaceful soul he has always been.

The legal system, the plant officials, or really anyone else of seemingly "worthless" power, to Nuke, couldn't seem to pry his heart away from what truly matters. He suffers terribly as he cries while being bathed very carefully, as his black skin that had been burned so badly, which had come into full contact with the spilt nuclear waste, screamed in absolute undefined agony, but through it all Nuke seemed to be taking it quite well. The man was not able to rise up from his hospital bed, as not only because he was a safety risk, but because of the extensive brain damage he sustained from the radiation poisoning, as well as from his fall that had mildly fractured his skull. Nuke was a very gentle man, and he appeared serene although this was certainly not a place where serenity resides to staying. However there is most certainly something lurking inside of Nuke Wilcox that is vibrant and far from being labeled as something ephemeral, but rather permanent. Nuke harbored sadness, however, as psychiatrists who visited him were able to vaguely sensate. However, Nuke merely stated that he was not really ready to "plunge back into the nuclear waste" just yet.

What was surprising to these professionals who deal specifically with victims of nuclear disasters like Nuke, was that this seemingly mild mannered, and even 'gentle" man, was barely manifesting any symptomology of trauma, although he has certainly talked about it over and over again. His parents talk with these same professionals as well as his special team of physicians, and they too make certain that it is known about they're son's resiliency. He speaks rather gently with the priests who are mostly here to administer the last rites in the final hours or days of these poor people who come here from nuclear accidents and only to die, but rather Nuke somehow chose to remain living, which defies medical understanding. But the priests convey to the physicians as well as to Nuke's parents that, "he is obviously protected by the grace of God, and that Nuke contains something within him which relieves him of worry or fear of the state of existence called death."

Nuke laments about his life at home as he never moved out to live on his own, but rather he remained with his parents in the rural community in the state of Tennessee. No longer does he work in the "Sequoya" power plant and talks daily with his closest friends. His damage that was the byproduct of the fall as well as the spill of the raw liquid nuclear waste happened so quickly, like all things in life that alter one's very existence in a catastrophic manner, had been far from brief as well as something easily remedied. He was tested in ways that could not have been done when he absorbed the extensive amount of nuclear radiation, so an M.R.I. was performed. What had been discovered was that the left hemisphere of the limbic system, which is on either side of the brain and is closest to the temple, but on the side of the head, and is responsible for some of our emotions, as this literally merges through the temporal lobe, has been damaged severely. As if Nuke was no longer truly capable of experiencing some of our deepest emotions, this connection had been almost completely severed from the fall as the man hit his head very hard, but the impact was much harder than they earlier suspected. Also from the excessive and literally lethal exposure to this radiation, as well as the nuclear waste itself, a great deal of brain tissues have been destroyed to no return, meaning Nuke could never be rehabilitated if life expectancy had not eluded him. Right now, two months after this terrible accident, Nuke Wilcox was still able to effectively communicate very well, but the man was unable to phonotate, or shape his mouth to make particular sounds that promote adequate speech, hence he spoke very morbidly-his words were garbled and came out with agonizing pain as he attempted to move his poor mouth that was completely paralyzed on one side-his left. This is what Cellia, Nuke's mother meant when she first saw his face from behind the lead glass of his room and said to her husband, "There is something wrong with him."

Nuke appeared to be detached form the world around him upon first glance, but this statement is far from any truth. He is very acute and knowing of all that is going on around him as he hears people like him, usually victims of radiation sickness, crying out in agonizing pain, while one night, a fellow victim next door rattled his final breaths with a nurse present as she attempted to help him feel less fearful. Nuke mentioned to his parents and friends from the power plant, that he felt sad for them. "I know my time is soon to come too, but I don't know when my radiation sickness will decide to take me home." ,Nuke said in his slow and labored speech. His movements are very jerky as they are labored, but he does not really know what he is doing half the time. However, his childlike character has certainly won him notoriety here with the nursing staff as they really cared for Nuke, but in a way that far supersedes any other patient they have ever had here. The manner he speaks to them when he was awake as they entered his room to care for his constant needs. They all kiddingly tell him it is like entering a nuclear power plant, because of the numerous metal signs placed all about the walls. These rooms usually do not provide a television, but his parents brought in his own form home, which he certainly appreciated as the days would be so long that he would actually cry, and bitterly.

When the nursing staff cared for Nuke's needs, it was like caring for a baby, because of not only the manner in which he now spoke as the byproduct of the terrible accident, but because the man was so gentle and profoundly tolerant, as well as secretly needful of their touch as it was well reflective of his mother a long time ago during his boyhood. Only now he is a man, but a dying man who was once a very gifted individual who worked proudly, but humbly for twenty-one years at the nuclear power plant handling nuclear waste. He made many good friends along the way, and these same friends reveal just how much he has meant to them by coming well over one-hundred miles every few weeks to sit by his bedside for hours and talk or just to be there by his wavering side, and to tacitly reveal to this same gentle and kind man who was slowly dying from severe radiation sickness, that he is loved and will never be forgotten, as he made the power plant a happier place because he was there with them. (If one wants to call a place as this happy.)

The prolonged sessions at court, which were not televised, but forwarded exclusively by the vigilant media, had more than obviously taken it's toll on the couple, especially concerning the knowledge that had come to them from seemingly out of nowhere about "bogus" files that were most definitely fabricated about they're son. The "Department of Energy" desperately made it's rebuttal avidly known to all within the courtroom as well as to the regional newspapers in the area. Nuke Wilcox is certainly no nuclear terrorist, but merely someone who prefers to keep by himself during times when no work was available. The young man busted his "ass" every day for the power plant that more than obviously never really cared for him in the first place. "Nuke" was not present to defend himself, but his parents had clearly done they're utmost to persuade the jury, as well as anyone there who would listen, that they're son was simply a gentle childlike man who loved working in the nuclear power plant that supplied electrical energy to all regions throughout the area. He was only a man who lead a simple existence, and who unknowingly touched the lives of most who worked along side him, as well as those who had not. "Nuke" has a mannerism that won him a gentle form of recognition and never caused anyone to worry about him being labeled as a terrorist, which to everyone in the courtroom, by now, completely believed this bogus information as ludicrous, and nothing short of it. In fact, papers following the high profile court case had written clearly in their captions as well as articles, "This had surely got to be the most outrageous propaganda since the communist invasion into our American soil during the Second World War and the cold war. How can one simple man, who is not even present, defend himself from such incredulous fascists who clearly have nothing better to do than to foolishly blame someone for being a terrorist, but this same power plant hired the youth twenty-one years ago as soon as he graduated from college? Okay officials, so high and mighty; tell us just what this poor dying man has supposed to have done to you're precious power plant?"

Eventually things were straightening out, but it was mostly due to the genuine assistance provided to them by the "Department of Energy," as these caring representatives who stood by the Wilcox's on a personal level, oversaw everything, and were most definitely affected by what they saw, as well as heard from not only their clients, which are the parents of the victim, but from the defense as well. They were more than stymied by the overall sense of malice and uncaring attitudes that were perpetuated through this case that grew more and more misleading as time went on. There was so much conjecture amidst their pomp and malicious behavior which the Judge and the jury could very easily hear, that the true nature of this trial was being overshadowed by it. However the Department managed to get things placed back into perspective, as it was to no avail that a man was almost brutally killed by an accident that was obviously done by human error although robots are lastly responsible for welding these canisters shut, because of the high levels of nuclear radioactivity, but although these robots had done the final job as stated, it was still considered as gross negligence, because humans program and operate these machines which the whole nuclear power plant depends on. The floor had been priorly inspected as mentioned, but time had lapsed in between this mentioned inspection, and cracks and small ruts formed in the concrete floor that carried the footsteps of Nuke Wilcox that fateful day that now dwells in an isolated and eternally sorrowful infamy for the loving parents. They're adult child lies in a radiation, or nuclear victim care facility for the rest of his life, as what had been recently explained to them before this particular day at court, that Nuke needs round the clock care and no nursing home facility is equipped or trained to handle cases as these, hence he must remain here. Nuke had this same tragic information explained to him as well, but surprisingly he took it rather well, but deep inside he was eternally crying, which was something that could most definitely be seen by the eyes of not only his caring parents who loved him so, but the nursing staff who also cared about him, but equally in an emotional manner. He has touched the personal lives of so many because of his gentleness and how he carries deeply within, a form of inner strength that was far from being labeled something as inert, or useless, but was rather candid and lasting as it emanated from every part of his being and soul.

The "Department of Energy" personally went to the distraught couple who were lost in a sea of ever building tears, because they knew that Nuke's time was drawing closer and closer every day that lapses, and the officials at the "Sequoya" power plant aren't making things easier in the slightest. The parents of this innocent and kind young man, who had fallen victim to a devastating accident involving a spill of deadly nuclear waste amidst transferring, faced each day with dread as well as thankfulness that Nuke was still alive and coherent. However Cellia, the mother of Nuke, cried uncontrollably during her times at court, at home by her husband's side, and of course, while visiting they're son. She, like her husband, was an emotional wreck as four months have slowly gone by to prove something that is so easy to comprehend, even by the publics' standards. In fact, the general public in the state of Tennessee became latently outraged and congregated around the courthouse as well as coming as close to the gates of the "Sequoya" nuclear power plant as possible without being arrested. They shouted slogans of angry protest over the terrible fate of the young victim, the young man, who now no longer works in the place of public service he loved, but rather is now fighting for his life as he was burned in various places beyond recognition, but luckily he was wearing the lead lined suit correctly as he has always done, hence what saved him from anything worse. In the meantime, Nuke saw something on the daily news flashing on the screen of his television about himself, which at first made him shiver, but then after a few hours made him smile. Nuke was a very humble man, as well as a God fearing man, who was raised with traditional values. His already quieted self became more so upon seeing things as this on T.V. He was very, very sick and was slowly dying, but still his specialized physicians in this field of medicine had no tangible reasoning behind his seemingly miraculous survival.

Friends came to visit Nuke and had taken photos on a digital camera that requires a computer to process and print the pictures, but one could already see what the final product was going to look like prior. These said pictures were taken by a very close friend of Nuke who was a fellow handler of nuclear waste, but for some reason that was completely unknown to anyone, including the man who had long befriended Nuke, was respected more and was thought highly of. He was touched by what happened to Nuke as tears often fall from his eyes while talking to the poor man now lying here by his side, as he was also the one who had given him the most signs form the power plant. The photos were of bright colors and one could genuinely see the horrific results of what happened at the site of the accident that never should have happened. Nuke's burns were healing, but this was because of the extensive care he was receiving as this was also a normal regimen when helping a victim of radiation poisoning or some other accident involving the latter. Amidst all of this high profiled hubbub in the courts, here at the facility things were quiet and very thought provoking. Sadness engulfed the heart and soul of Nuke, but again he never liked to reveal too much of this side of himself, as he was never really that kind of person to do so. He was very private, especially because he was very lonely all of his existence although he never once let on to anyone, save for his parents who had already well known this to be highly true, but they too just could not understand it, especially where he was such a caring person who was considerate of the feelings of others around him and he tried to help out in any way he could, like making newcomers feel welcomed; both at school and at the nuclear power plant. However through all of this, Nuke never at all blamed anyone for what has happened to him, which was surprisingly unbelievable in the eyes of psychology, physiology, and the thanotologists, or grief counselors who talk with the dying or to the bereaved. Many loving attempts were tried to make Nuke come to better terms with his plight that will eventually take away his young life, but he never budged. Nuke only told them in his wavering and gentle voice that was temporarily interrupted by an involuntary smile or open mouth followed by silence, "I', the...the one who fell in the nuclear waste...it was no one's fault. It was just as accident. I don't mind what happened to me....No...I'm not...not afraid to die. I like living here with all...all of my...my...my fellow "nukes." Ha, ha, ha, ha.....Nukes." ,Nuke softly explained while lying here in his hospital bed and being eternally fed through his intravenous PICC line inserted deeply inside of his arm and into the inferior vena cava of the heart. His bald head reflected the mode of deterioration his body was enduring from such an horrific misfortune. Gentle and quiet, but happy, as his childlike nature he was born with exuded through his speech, except for very select times while talking with someone about particular genre.` However Nuke was here in his own room and listened to his tapes brought in from his parents as he listened to them on his head phones and mildly rocked to the music playing loudly in his ears like a big teenager. He listened to groups like "Megadeath," "Nuclear Assault," "Morbid Angel," "Cannibal Corpse," 'Ozzy Osbourne," etc. Sometimes he would try to sing out with them, but his voice was mutilated and profoundly weak, yet he was admired for his loving attempt to remain that person he was before being destroyed by a spilt barrel of raw nuclear waste. In fact Nuke often says out loud for no apparent reasoning, "nuclear waste," but in a very sad, almost mournful tone, as if crying out for help, but no one knows this, nor does the poor man himself, although he is often heard all hours of the day and into the quiet, but sometimes stressful nights here, but certainly not in the life of Nuke Wilcox, but rather in those of his fellow victims, as the nights are sometimes broken with piercing alarms of warning or indication that a patient's life is in danger and everyone on staff rushes to aid with carts full of medical supplies to try to save these poor patients who's lives will truly never be. Nuke's gaunt face full of burns on either of his cheeks suddenly become moistened with a stream of warm silent tears as he realizes his day is going to come, but when? When' Lord? When?

It was obviously beyond evident that the "Sequoya" nuclear power plant was completely at fault for this poor man's terrible damage as well as for his premature death that is soon to come, but no one really knows just when it will happen. By the time this tedious and highly emotionally charged case ended, the Tennessee "Department of Energy" had assisted the Wilcox's to not only win they're settlement in the name of they're only son, but they won a cash lump sum of one million dollars in the process. In the meantime, the leading officials at the power plant had not much to say to the public media concerning this case, which inside sources believe, they knew their claims regarding "Nuke" would eventually be discovered as highly irrational and bogus. However something of utter sorrowful and even surprising consequence happened when his parents went to the facility where Nuke was residing for the rest of his natural life, because when Nuke was told about the court case and the million dollar settlement given to them from the Federal aid of the "Department of Energy," the poor man actually cried, but not with joy, but rather with great sadness. He told his parents that it was wrong to take the plant to court and steal money form them, when it was all his fault. To put it bluntly, Nuke was angry at his loving parents, but unbeknown to the distraught young man, this was won for him, because of the terrible fact that he had been catastrophically damaged from this industrial accident at the plant. It took some time to get this once problematic idea into his head that was more than obviously damaged from this accident.

Nuke talked a lot with his mother as well as his father while it was safe for them to enter his room. They would sit together on his bed at the edge and gently embrace the poor man who was emaciating before they're very eyes. They had to explain things slower than before his falling to the floor and the spill of the nuclear waste, but it mattered not to them, because of they're love for the man was redundant as it was everlasting. His cheeks were gaunt and badly blackened from coming into contact with the liquid nuclear waste that had seeped into his lead lined suit, which made him look more "old" appearing. Nuke understood what his parents told him, but he was a gentle minded man who has never really wanted to interfere with things that he believes are "none of his business." His parents diligently attempted to explain to this poor damaged man that this money was compensation for all of his horrific suffering, which Nuke himself had no real tangible idea as to how much he, himself has endured and will later. He does know that he is dying, which secretly makes him very, very sad, but Nuke equally understands with the greatest form of joy humanly possible, and that he will receive his reward in Heaven with the love and grace of the All Mighty God. His voice was labored as it was wracked with pain, because only half of his face was moving, but his string of caring physicians talk respectfully with the poor man about his condition, as things sometimes needed to be repeated in order for him to understand.

His parents had a lot to say in regards to the court case, especially pertaining to the leading officials at the "Sequoya" nuclear power plant.

FATHER, Jake Wilcox; "This shows their guilt. They were arrogant as they were uncaring about what happened to our son who was so badly damaged from this industrial accident. How in God's name can people exist in places as these? Our son is dying of advanced radiation sickness that is so severe, that it is nothing short of a miracle he is still here with us. That power plant is full of cowards who refuse to take responsibility for their actions and simply admit they screwed up."

MOTHER, Cellia Wilcox: "Nuke" was so brave as he is loving. Everyone of his colleagues loved him as some even drive that long distance to see him every once in a while. They talk about the plant, as "Nuke" always laments on the fact that he can never go back there. He says that the spill never deterred him from wanting to go back and do it all over again. His spirit is so strong, and that's why I believe he is still alive. 9She begins to cry momentarily, but then continues speaking.)...I wish that he could only just come home. (Sob, sob.)

FATHER, Jake Wilcox: "Nuke" is really a "sweet" gut, which sounds strange when describing a man this way. He was very shy with girls while growing up in his world of intelligible silence, but they were still drawn to him just the same. He was quiet like he is right now; really smart, loving, and compassionate, as well as overwhelmingly accepting of what has happened to him, which includes his advanced radiation sickness. Nuke loves anything "nuclear," as his room is filled with signs of all sizes of the universal symbol, or what he prefers to call the "nuclear wheel." But now with the help of his many friends at the plant, his room at the radiation care facility is filled with these huge metal signs all around his bed on the walls as there is no window there, which I believe, doesn't help him any, but he loves it-even after this terrible fate that now looms over him. Our son is a wonderful, kind, and very brave young man who didn't even want us to go to court, as he insists that the industrial accident was his fault alone, and not the plant's. The "Department of Energy" won us a settlement of one million dollars in monetary compensation, but when my wife and I told Nuke he was not in the least bit interested about the money. Instead we have so far used some of it to pay back the lawyers, and on a little research for the better treatment of nuclear victims like our son, especially those involved in nuclear accidents; again, like our son."

SPOKESPERSON FOR THE "DEPARTMENT OF ENERGY" : "It was absolutely disgusting....absolutely disgusting....Neither one of us from the Department could believe our eyes when we first came upon this case of severe negligence that is so beyond description and excuse, we didn't quite know what to make of it. We still cannot believe, although some time has gone by, that the officials of this plant, with a spotless reputation for safety and the following of other vitally important responsibilities, refuse at all costs to simply sat to these people they made a mistake.

They were terrible towards this suffering family of a poor dying young man as they actually snubbed them in the midst of they're tremendous psychological pain. I mean, they're son is in a facility for radiation sickness that is very advanced from this reckless and inexcusable accident. No one took the slightest responsibility for their actions and screw up's-we couldn't believe it, and neither could the attorneys, which included those for the defense. I mean, what is the matter with these people?!....We personally went to bat for this family while the plant officials were doing everything they possibly could to sweep it all under the rug and hope it will go away, like Nuke will eventually, but the "Sequoya" power plant had another thing coming. They were slapped hard with numerous regulations failures and citations that will never go away. This man's family, or his parents, as well as the man himself, the victim, must be compensated somehow, and we managed to at least do something worthwhile for them to ease such suffering."

INVESTOGATOR FOR THE "DEPARTMENT OF ENERGY"/ NUCLEAR MATERIALS: "We worked exclusively for a long time with the photos taken of the scene where the victim fell, as well as of the actual barrel itself, which most definitely concluded that the welding used in the process of closure of these canisters by robots that become stronger with time, was not thoroughly configures by whoever it was who claimed the task of running and programming these robots. It was also highly seen during inspection amidst this concrete floor, although in good condition and well maintained, was still not well inspected as we later discovered other cracks here as well, but were luckily more away from the scene where the spill had originated. If someone asked me again if I believed this accident was the fault of the "Sequoya" power plant? Yes; I'd have to say it, because it is. This man's life was destroyed with radiation sickness that is taking away his life as I speak, but no one knows as to just how long it will take, because he is such a fighter, as he is the only recorded person in the history of nuclear accidents and disasters who has survived an exposure of over 500 R.E.M.'S, which is literally impossible, as death is immanent in either days or even hours. The burns have healed quite a bit since I have seen him in person at the nuclear care facility, but things are not going to be as good for this power plant as it's reputation will probably never be trusted again, especially by us in the Department. As the "Department of Energy," we are the watchdogs in the nuclear world here on this earth, and if we discover gross behaviors like what we were called into, then these institutions get barked at, but more than this, they eventually get bitten, and quite badly I must add. What has happened here at this power plant is inexcusable and I am beyond surprised with the lack of ethics displayed from these leading officials who still adamantly refuse to comment, as they even have the fortitude to squeak out to the immediate family with a completely false apology. I for one, was disgusted beyond belief, especially when it was also discovered these officials on the board at the plant were receiving monetary kickbacks as they were buying people off after the accident involving this poor defenseless victim as he lies in a radiation victim care facility waiting to die and while doing so, he is suffering the tortures of Hell. We at the Department will not stand for it, and if they continue to be guilty of subversive behaviors like this, then we will have to shut them down. We have been watching them at the "Sequoya' power plant like a starving coyote ever since this industrial accident that happened about four months ago, as this said accident should never have happened. NEVER."

MOTHER, Cellia Wilcox: "The "Department of Energy" was so nice to us as well as to our son. They treated us with real compassion and our terrible situation with a loving concern, which I have never heard of before when concerning accidents involving nuclear energy or materials, or whatever...I also know "Nuke" appreciates what they have personally done for him too."

FATHER. Jake Wilcox: "You know, surprisingly, "Nuke" was not too grieved over what has happened to him-it seems to me anyway. I have always believed that he has something in him that just emanates from his soul that is good, but not to be considered as "run of the mill" good....Nuke is very accepting of his sudden illness as well as what happened to him, because of the spill of the nuclear waste falling on him. The specialized people who talk with "Nuke" say to us that he is thoroughly at peace with what he will eventually go through; his death. But, what they cannot understand as well as us as his parents, is that Nuke does not blame the plant, or anyone there. He also enjoys living at the facility, but he would occasionally like to visit home again, and to drive by the power plant where he worked for years...As his parent I just can't quite understand it, but I sure do love him, and I'll never forget what he looked like when we fist saw him just hours after the terrible accident. Oh, God...(Sigh)..."Nuke" was lying there on his back in the room he now lives in; all burned black and wrapped in burn cloths. He was on oxygen and I.V's placed into his arm, as it was a cathider sticking from out of his upper left arm and it was attached to a bag filled with something to help his condition. Now he's shriveled up, emaciated with no hair on his head or anywhere on his poor body as we saw that same night when we were called to arrive...Oh, it was awful..."

MOTHER, Cellia Wilcox: "He now has brain damage from the massive overdose of nuclear radiation as well as from the fall as he hit his head so hard on the cement floor of the plant. Nuke moves very jerky and he cannot walk, so he is catheterized because he cannot rise without assistance. Nuke's words, although can be understood, are terribly mutilated and they sound as if they are "racked" with tremendous pain, as they no longer flow, but are severely labored. He sometimes stops in the midst of speaking and smiles involuntarily, as we found this is all from the massive overdoes of nuclear radiation that bombarded his brain as he lie in the nuclear waste spill that was displaced all around him. But he appears happy, especially when he talks to us about the plant, his friends at the plant; even the spill he loves to talk about-to simply tell his story to anyone who will listen."

FATHER, Jake Wilcox: "Yes, it's almost like his accident is a badge of honor for Nuke."

The subject of his radiation sickness came up, and it was hard for the nurse, as she truly "loved" this disabled man lying here before her in a completely helpless manner that required her very existence if he is to remain alive. The overall message shared between them was quite clear, and that be that this poor man was contented, but secretly saddened, yet again, the redundant emotion here was the former.

She had been called by her fellow nurse as a patient was in need of assistance down the long hall of the facility for these very special patients of industrial accidents. She gently tapped Nuke's left forearm, which was the one closest to her, and said that she would be seeing him throughout the day until 4:00 p.m. Suddenly all was serenely calm and quiet as Nuke felt a little better on the internal. His badly disabled hands, all curled up but were still mobile, save for his left, cradled the remote control to his television brought to him from home some months back. He was still in the original uprighted position the caring nurse had placed his bed in order to give him the medicine he required each day. The television warmed up momentarily and the news came on and a calm moan emerged from this kind and gentle wounded man who was so badly disfigured and burned from the barrel of raw untreated liquid nuclear waste falling around him. He would sometimes look down at his poor body that was victimized by the field he loves more than anything in existence, save for other things that meant so much more to him, like his family, the earth, the needs of people, and most of all, his God. Speaking of God, Father Jason walks into the room of this gentle victim. Nuke says a weak and labored "Hello." Father Jason knew Nuke very well and has always been profoundly affected by not only what has happened to him, but overall his wondrous achievement of enlightenment that he has possessed long before ever getting into this traumatic situation.

He asks Nuke if he would like to have Communion, and of course, Nuke replies "Oh, yes." Father Jason smiles, because he has already known ahead of time that this man in particular would always wish to receive it. He explained earlier to Nuke that most people here are too sick to even want the Holy Eucharist, or simply don't want it, but Nuke's understanding, although was now waning, could not comprehend such a blasphemed thing. He had been asked by the Father if he would like him to turn down the sound of his T.V. but Nuke, in his labored and painful sounding voice, expressed something on the contrary, which was this, "No...I'll turn it off...I don't want to destroy the sacredness of this moment that should be cherished at all times." Tears fell from Father Jason's kindly eyes, as he has never once met a patient, as well as any layman for that matter, who feels as well as can express such genuine love and faith. The rather young, but middle aged priest administered the Holy Eucharist to Nuke and he gently placed the bread into the quivering mouth of this dying victim. Tears now rolled down the badly burned cheeks of this gentle man who was so fatally ill from the severe and advanced radiation sickness that is eventually going to take him away from them.

Nuke thanked Father Jason and said it was "good." The priest smiled and replied, "I'm glad it was good, Nuke. You have so much faith in a way I have never seen before...I feel like I have been blessed by knowing you." Nuke smiled in his childlike way, but he replied to the man of God tenderly, "I'm just a man who got nuclear.....radioactive.... I have radiation sickness. I'm radioactive from falling with a barrel of nuclear waste...nuclear waste." Father Jason knew and agreed about the affects of this accident that is now literally killing him by degrees, but certainly not in regards to his worth. He sat down and spoke more depthfully to this poor man about how he has told his fellow priests about him, which meant that he was sharing to these men about Nuke's wondrous and inspiring religious faith that is truly wondrous as it is childlike, which is how it is supposed to be. Father Jason admitted his truest testimony to this man lying beside him in a hospital bed, and that was, that he had given so much to this place, which is mostly a place of death and horrific despair, but when he came along, Nuke's gentle acceptance of the death that looms consistently over him had certainly won the hearts of nearly everyone who works here. "By being yourself, Nuke, you have touched the lives of so many here and in ways you probably cannot yet imagine. You are a beautiful man, Nuke. You are beautiful." Suddenly, Nuke spoke candidly to Father Jason, but he was very sad as his overall mood had altered consistently. Nuke said in his tremendously arduous speech, "I'm not beautiful...I'm all burned form the nuclear waste. I'm ugly...I was destroyed by nuclear waste...I loved nuclear waste and it hurt me. But I don't blame the plant. It was my fault.....I'm not beautiful, I'm ugly." Tears were now falling from his eyes as they stung his face as he couldn't stand anything touching this part of his body, as he would moan out in pain. Father Jason was deeply moved by this man's candor and honesty. However, the caring priest told Nuke that he really was beautiful, and it had not mattered what he looks like, but rather what dwells on the inside of us that makes an unattractive person beautiful, even a victim of a nuclear accident like his. Nuke cried, but quietly as he admitted to Father Jason that he was dying from radiation sickness. "I'm in so...so much pain from being nuclear." ,Nuke explained sorrowfully. Father Jason hugged Nuke carefully as Nuke returned his same emotion to this kindly man of God. He began to cry while feeling that most truthful benefaction of being a recipient of God's sacred and redeeming love. Nuke was acknowledged by these priests here as one who has been truly blessed with many gifts of rare understanding as well as conceptions that so very few will ever understand as well as achieve, meaning a piece of mind that can only be gotten by knowing God in a rare manner. It was obviously clear to them as well as the Clergy, that Nuke Wilcox was crying out, but he didn't quiet know how to ask for help or for something which he did not know existed within himself at this particular time in his suddenly shortened life span. He was dying right before their eyes, and his fellow patients at this specialized care facility were trying to not only befriend to make him happier and comfortable, but once truly knowing this gentle man, it became easier as well as something that was considered as "joyful." Nuke said to Father Jason before he left his room to go to other fellow patients, "The heart if restless until it rests in Christ.."

Father Jason turned and smiled brightly and agreed to the words of such honesty and loving truth that fell so easily from this poor damaged man. Nuke was again by himself as he turned on his television once more and watched some cartoons for a laugh. The many metal signs that had been brought into his room by a friend who worked with Nuke at the power plant appeared to watch him in a manner that eluded his now insidiously clouding psyche as the affects of his radiation sickness, especially the man's inability to even put his words together in normally sounding sentences. Sooner or later, he will barely be able to talk as well as breathe on his own. Only the Lord God knows what is now to befall this humble and shy man with the nickname "Nuke."

Back at the "Sequoya" nuclear power plant that was closer to his home and his parents, two men are seated together in a rather quieted lounge in the upstairs part of the plant. One of them was Bob, the friend who had brought Nuke most of the large metal signs from the plant, and another man sat next to him who was not quite as close to Nuke, but knew this poor man rather well. They were having hot coffee and talking about the tragic news about they're companion in the Tennessee newspapers in the area, and especially about what the "Department of Energy" had later discovered upon further inspection of files concerning employees who worked here. What had been avidly on the agenda of their discussion, as well as of those who worked at this same power plant, as even those who had not known Nuke, were absolutely stymied at the information in pertinence to Nuke Wilcox as him being labeled as a nuclear terrorist, which was absolutely absurd. However what was being spoken of right now was the condition of Nuke, as Bob was the one who had spent the most time visiting the man personally since this accident which has now occurred close to five months ago. Worry as well as a very real sadness plagued these people, especially those now seated here in the smaller lounge that was located upstairs. Bob was the one who had taken many digital photographs of their friend back at the radiational care facility located in the near center of the state. He carried two particular ones with him at all times so he could see the face of his true friend all of the time, which was something that had given him comfort that he truly needed. All of the employees here at the "Sequoya" nuclear power plant had been undoubtedly emotionally affected and were required to see a specially trained psychiatrist to assist them through the tragedy that had caused not only most of the plant to evacuate, due to the extensive radiation leak that spilled out into the environment, but all people who lived in the vicinity of the first mile and a half, so as not to be exposed to this fatal level of nuclear radiation as the lethality of the background radiation from the spilled waste is certain. Suddenly, a "suit," or a representative entered the rather quiet scene of the employees' lounge and interrupted the small talk shared by these two caring men in reference to their friend. The other man was told to go back to work, while Bob was instructed to come with him and follow to the head office that was located away from the actual working areas of the plant.

Bob was frightened, but like the man he is, he remain levelheaded in an otherwise chaotic situation as he wondered if his job was suddenly at stake, but as for the reasoning, he claimed no idea, but the worry for his friend Nuke, was the redundant subject locked tightly within his mind and heart at this moment.

Bob was told to come onto the plush office and take a seat. There was no one else there, so his previous uptight nerves suddenly calmed themselves a bit, but still as to why he was here, the reason had not yet manifested itself. The office was almost a luxury place where a wet bar was present as well as other things that make a representative's life more "cushy." The man, Mr. Claude Foster, was one of the head executives of the board for the power plant and was also highly guilty concerning everything about Nuke's otherwise subversively bogus file that was placed as a "dummy" to hide the otherwise "gentle" truth about this same man. He spoke to Bob about the signs, as it was discovered a while back that he had been seen stealing them one by one off the walls. He had been told that where these signs were new, the money was going out of his paycheck, which would total to about $700.00, but Bob testified to Mr. Foster that he would gladly pay for them right now out of his wallet. However Mr. Foster refused to negotiate with this man, in fact, it was told to Bob that if he does not agree to have his payment partially revoked until the signs were paid for in full, he loses his job here at the plant. Bob did not wish to lose his position here, although he hated what happened in secret as well as the actual accident that never at all should have happened in the first place. Bob already had his wallet out of the back pocket, but unknowingly his two photos of Nuke had fallen to the rug before the desk which was a rather large space. Mr. Foster wanted to see these photos, but Bob only stated to him that they were only shots of Nuke which he had taken while visiting him at the facility where he had been airlifted that day and now resides. Still, the official wanted to see them. In fact, he demanded. Bob handed them over immediately and without question.

Bob gave them to Mr. Foster and he looked at them, but suddenly a lapse of uncomfortable silence crept between them. The man then grasped tighter the edges of these two photos as something within the plant official began to emerge, but from deeply within. Bob stared intently at the official from across the wide space that spanned between them in this silent office. The man then shook momentarily from seeing what actually transpired here at this nuclear power plant from the spill. His heart then fluttered, but he suddenly, without forewarning, returned the photographs to Bob. Bon asked him if he was all right, because the whole atmosphere had become tense, but not so much in a manner of anger, but rather was consistent of a deep seated guilt. Mr. Foster wiped his forehead that began to heavily perspire. He gestured Bob to leave the office and to expect the money used to pay for the numerous signs he stole from this place to be removed from his weekly pay checks. Bob quickly stood up and turned around to leave when he looked back to where he had just been. He saw Mr. Foster seated awkwardly in his chair with one hand completely over his face and tears were falling from his shielded eyes. Bob was mildly gladdened at this reaction, although silently perceived, was still a reaction as just noted. Bob then left the office and walked silently, and almost gingerly, through the maze of halls and catwalks until he arrived back to his destination, which was back at the reactor monitoring station with his colleagues. One of them asked where he was, but Bob only softly replied, "I was in someone's office." He sat down to check the core temperature of the number 1 reactor, but his mind was still back in the office of this plant official. Scratching his neck, Bob then realized that Mr. Foster, a real hard case, was profoundly affected by what he saw, which was really a good thing, especially where it just may change things around here where it concerned people like Nuke, who handled the nuclear waste, which without individuals like him, there would be no power plants. Indeed a double edged dagger whenever concerning something like this, but nonetheless Nuke was tacitly affecting one of the leading officials of this place, and what better person to do that than Mr. "Nuke" Wilcox.

Chapter Eight

AT THE "SEQUOYA" POWER plant where this terrible and inexcusable accident transpired, the plant official known only as Mr. Foster, lamented furiously over the hideous and tragic sight he had seen with the power of the camera. The photos were now back in Bob's hands, but the memory of them literally burned their images in his mind as clear as the morning sky. He suddenly became completely silent and only spoke whenever needed, which had been immediately noticed here at this hectic and busy place of industry. There was one of the top officials who entered the office of Mr. Foster and he discussed his noticing of the man's sudden vow of silence. He wanted to known why, but his request to know was not in the least bit kind or reflective of compassion. It was all business and that was all, which was exactly what had been redundantly manifested in court and in front of the Tennessee "Department of Energy" as well as the parents of the poor victim.

Mr. Foster explained that he accidentally happened to see two digital photos of Nuke Wilcox in his bed at the nuclear victim care facility shortly after the accident. The top official replied uncaringly, "Yes, so...does that mean you've gone soft?" Bending over closer to make his presence and hollow authority known to Mr. Foster, he continued, "Nuke was a drone; a toxic waste worker. He wasn't that important-he was someone who can be easily replaced. You can't let this get to you...you have to understand that this is a place of business." Mr. Foster stood up and went to his wet bar, but only to get himself a glass of cold water, because he was sweating so profusely. He finally said to the top plant official, "We were wrong....If you only saw what I saw...(Sigh)...He was all burned, all of his hair was gone, and he was emaciated-deteriorating before my eyes, although it was in pictures. He's dying of radiation sickness, but I never saw it before...We were dead wrong to ignore those people; no wonder the Department is literally living here. We made it so tough for that man's parents, it made no sense-you kept saying to us, "Don't worry, it will all blow over...we can pay people off without the Department even knowing." All I can say is, we're so lucky the F.B.I. didn't get in on this, or we wouldn't have an ass left to sit on-" (He was cut off.) "All right...knock it off. You're getting yourself into a frazzle-look at you-you're a shaking, sweating mess. If you don't settle down, you're going to have another heart attack." ,the top plant official expressed while now standing up to leave the office. In the meantime, Mr. Foster was holding onto the glad made of lead crystal and leaning against the wall that was close to his desk. He took from out of his trousers' pocket a handkerchief and wiped his round face as it was literally saturated with sweat. He replied, "Yeah...I do feel weird." He sat himself down once more to rest. The top plant official replied coldly, "Don't tell anyone that you've seen those pictures of Nuke, or the whole plant could crumble down. I mean it. This case is closed...CLOSED." He pointed sternly at Mr. Foster prior to leaving the office. Now shutting the door he again left this distraught official very worried, but in a manner that was the cause of something decaying inside him. Guilt had most definitely surpassed any other of his emotions in pertinence to this extremely subversive situation, which even he had not been able to understand as to why Nuke was the scapegoat in the first place. He was just a simple humble man who worked daily for the power plant, and right from college, so how could he be all of those ridiculous things that he had been earlier claimed to be? What were these officials hiding? No matter what, he knew he had to calm himself down before something happens. Still, worry plagued this man because he couldn't figure why no one at this plant cared. He was literally drowning in sea of guilt, because he knew well that they could have done so much for this dedicated young man who has never been a problem, but perhaps considered a little odd at times, but that certainly poses no reasoning to condemn someone and recreate their life. Mr. Foster couldn't imagine the suffering this poor kind man has been enduring, which was highly considered a very truthful speculation. No one could personally imagine what it is like to be victimized by nuclear radiation or substances of a like nature, and nevermind radiation sickness that is so severe, it is nothing short of a miracle he even lived this long, especially concerning his brain functions, which were now slowly declining as all noticed right away.

His parents were told.

Yes, his parents.

They had been taken gently aside to explain that Nuke has to have his stomach removed in a couple of days from the affects of the advanced radiation sickness, which is now taking it's traumatic toll on the man's system. It had already been noticed by his folks that Nuke's brain functions have waned somewhat, and that eventually the worst is yet to come. The couple embraced each other tightly while they sat and waited for the figurative atomic bomb to drop, nevermind the rhetorical "fallout."

The very compassionate medical doctors who cared for people in situations like they're son, and who worked very hard to acquire this specialized medical Degree, as it is a highly special form of medicine, were here for this older couple in more ways than the customary norms. Meaning, as the Wilcox's sat in the office that held three doctors of this team, there was also a females counselor who was ready to explain particulars if deemed necessary. What had been explained to them, was that the excessive amount of nuclear radiation they're son's body and brain had absorbed was, by far, the worst case they have ever personally run against, save for a select few in industrial accidents as these that come from power plants, or in nuclear waste Federalized dumping grounds. They explained that it is rare to be exposed to this extremely high level of radiation, and nevermind having raw nuclear waste spill on the body's skin, and still be alive and consciously aware of one's environment, and for this long a period, which so far had lapsed into the sixth month. "He will eventually grow more and more weak and unable to move at all, as his entire central nervous system will be tremendously compromised. Eventually Nuke won't be able to talk, as you can easily hear now. But the worst that will happen to him, is that he will no longer know you, as he will eventually fall into a deep coma and finally die." ,The doctors explained as gently as they could, but still despite it all, the truth emerged it's hideous and sorrowful head.

Mrs. Wilcox immediately cried bitterly, while her husband, with tears hanging in his own eyes, held his wife who was visibly shaking. The female counselor took hold of her hand that was free and held it caringly and told them that these people here and all over, will help to make him as comfortable as possible so his passing will not be as bad as it really is. Still it made no difference, as all of their cottling and gentle outreach will not remove the fact that Nuke is dying of radiation sickness from the industrial accident. She shook her fist and said, "That damn plant thinks it won...well, think again!" Cellia jumped up and ran out of the filled office; her husband excused himself and went after her.

The next day Nuke was wheeled to the regular area of the hospital, meaning there exists on the other side, a regular medical hospital, hence the reasoning for these rather large patches of a yellow background and there is a black "nuclear" symbol in the foreground to serve as a warning to employees that he is a "radiation care patient." He was very sad, but already well accustomed to not eating through his stomach, but still the prospects of it all frightened him. He had a rare string of drug allergies, which his system is now more sensitized, due to the radiation absorption. They were also going to perform a colonoscopy, but the scope was going to go through the entire length of the six feet of small intestines, hence as to why he was assisted in cleaning out the previous day. Nuke lie here waiting to be taken into the room where he will be completely sedated with the very drug he now uses on a day to day basis-Fentanyl, which is a pain killer as well as an anesthetic, along with Propofol, which is manufactured form egg whites, and is strictly a synthetic anesthetic. .

They were kind to Nuke, as all knew who he was by not only the news articles still occasionally broadcast, but from the talk amongst fellow medical doctors and other colleagues. Nuke was finally wheeled into the room which was really an operating room; Nuke was told by an anesthesiologist, that when he was taken here the night of the spill at the nuclear power plant, he was the one who worked with him. Nuke smiled like a child as they hooked up his dual lumen PICC line cathider with a liter of dextrose 0.5. He was cold, as it usually is in operating rooms, so in his mutilated voice he spoke up while everyone got the room and the patient ready for surgery and other testing. Nuke said, with a mutilated voice that appeared like a severely damaged man, which he now was, said to the caring and competent team, "I'm cold…Aaaahhhh." 'You're cold?' ,asked the assistant surgeon who came up to the edge of the operating table, "Okay, Nuke. We'll get you a couple of nice, warm blankets for you; how's that?" "Yeah." ,replied the gentle soul with a nod and a smile, but he shook from a mix of nerves and the cool temperature of the room. Warmed bedding was placed over the frailing body of Nuke. He cooed happily in reaction to the warmth as well as to their caring about his comfort, but he sensed in all ways of necessity. The drugs were now being administered, but he was told as was the rule of ethics concerning all conscious patients, whether they could understand or not. His heart skipped beats constantly as it was recently discovered he developed tangible heart disease from this exposure to the radioactive waste as well as to the radiation that bombarded his body. A cardiac drug had been pushed through his PICC line which almost immediately calmed the worsening symptomology, as they knew he just may suffer a heart attack by the hills and valleys appearing on the screen of the large monitor.

Nuke felt very peaceful as he preferred to feel. His words slurred excessively now that these anesthetics passed the blood brain barrier and calmed him as he was almost immediately in mid-conscious. The chief surgeon entered the room and saw Nuke and smiled, but he was so saddened by what he saw, especially concerning the patch symbol on his Johnny which "sang out" that he was a victim of radiation or other nuclear incidences. Nuke tried to say "hi," but the powerful drugs prohibited him from doing so. He soon went of to sleep and the surgeons went to work.

Nuke finally awakened on recovery and cried out in agony although he was given morphine before waking up. However Nuke's crying out was merely a mutilated and raspy prolonged moan, "Aaaaaahhhhhhh." The nurses came to Nuke and helped him with his needs. His Foley cathider bag had to be drained, as it was full from all of the fluids given to him. After that he fell back to sleep as he could certainly feel like something has been literally "removed," and it was; his stomach. Nuke was awakened by a surgeon who worked on him back in the O.R. Dr. Henkel explained that his stomach had been completely removed as they had hoped a small portion of it could be salvaged, but not so. Nuke asked what that "hissing" sound was. Dr. Henkel explained to Nuke that his mid abdomen, where the gut was once located, has a small tube inserted that is hooked up to a suction machine, called "lavage." He explained that after an organ like this is removed, for a time, usually a week, the cavity must be under constant suction to maintain good drainage of old blood form removal at surgery, as well as to keep the vacated area free from the build up of bacteria. He was pumped with power antibiotics through his PICC line, which to remind the reader is an implanted intravenous line that goes up into the inferior vena cava of the heart, as it is an access that is also used for home use or anywhere. Nuke was in very little pain, as it had been reassured to him that the suction was gentle, as it may feel like pressure, but that sensation was okay. Nuke still managed to understand the information the surgeon had given him. In the meantime, Nuke's parents were called to notify them the surgery was a success, but there was more bad news on the professional and personal agenda.

Over the telephone, Dr. Henkel explained not only what was done, and that they're son was doing well, they had discovered something in Nuke's bowels that was not an uncommon thing concerning someone who has endured severe radiation poisoning. Dr. Henkel told them both that Nuke's small intestines were rapidly deteriorating as the tissues were actually breaking down and would eventually, if he lives this long, which was highly doubtful, disintegrate. In other words, Nuke's body was doing just that. It has been going into the seventh month, but time has crawled by very slowly for not only the parents of this poor man, but for the victim as well. The tremendous psychological agony experienced and expressed by the couple, especially after hearing the furthered information by a very competent surgeon, caused them to suddenly stop living; as if the whole world had suddenly come to an immediate stop-like an entire world of screaming voices, then those screams are suddenly quelled into silence. The surgeon gave them his deepest sympathies possible, as even he too was holding back very human tears for this patient and his family. He recalled how compliant Nuke was as they prepped him for operating and further testing. He was happy and immediately accepting of not only before all of this, but after when he was told about the lavage, or constant suction of a hollow space or organ once either being removed, or worked on, to require good drainage while healing. He never even cried, reflected Dr. Henkel.

This same professional was also crying for this immediate family who more than obviously cherished him, as well as loved him. He hung up the telephone as he spoke to them in his personal office for privacy, especially where this news was so personal and terrible. Dr. Henkel took a moment before returning back to work and cried. Then, like a soldier briefly wounded during battle, opened his office door and walked back to the operating rooms to scrub for the next case, but fortunately, this caring surgeon has not had many "radiation victims" for a very long time, as they usually only come here to be operated on, but then die in a matter of hours or only days later.

Nuke was later taken to his room, but had awakened from his intensely drugged stupor. The nurses watched over him as they plugged in all of the equipment necessary to keep him alive and comfortable. Nuke said contentfully that he was "happy." One of the nurses who has witnessed many of these victim die right before her, bent over Nuke and gently attempted to stroke the side of his gaunt and burnt face. Nuke smiled his twisted smile, as it was this way, because of the paralyzation of his left side, but mostly in the head region of the body. Nuke winced out in pain, due to him not being able to stand anything against the tender skin that was scabbing over, but nonetheless it hurt very badly. Nuke moaned his long, raspy moans in reaction for most of his spoken words, "Aaaaahhhhhh." She replied gently, "Awe, does that hurt? Okay, I'm sorry, Honey. Are you all right for now? Do you want anything?" "No; I'm nuclear....nuclear." ,answered Nuke as he was not making much sense anymore. However he was very tired and closed his eyes, but then opened them once again and asked for his remote that was lying there on the table wheeled right up against the edge of his hospital bed. She barely understood him, but his words were figured out with a moment of contemplation. She gently handed it to Nuke's capable right hand, as she rearranged the call button closer in case he needed it, especially now. Nuke said lazily, "Thank you." "You're welcome, Sweety." Nuke then said to himself aloud while no one was there in his room as he watched the T.V. ,"nuclear waste....nuclear waste.....nuclear waste. Ha, ha, ha...I was radioactive." His voice was clearly reflective of a profoundly helpless and waning presence who now lies here waiting for the inevitable, but at the particular moment, or so it all appeared, contained no reactive emotions relative to just what happened as his stomach was completely taken, but moreover, the overall structural destruction of his entire bowels from being exposed to such a severely heightened level of nuclear radiation as well as the liquid nuclear waste which had spilled all around him and sifted into his lead lined suit, which was the very same the whole medical staff wore when receiving Nuke form the power plant after being airlifted here. As said, the kind and open anesthesiologist who spoke to Nuke, wore a suit like his own the same evening when he was called to assist with the 'stat" operation, which consisted of the removal of his thyroid, parathyroid, and some of his lymph glands.

Nuke was now sleeping as a good show he liked revealed itself on the screen, but the poor man only fell back to sleep form all of the drugs.

His parents came the following day to spend some time with him, but the poor young man was so out of it, he barely even acknowledged they were there. Nuke was not too sad right now, but he was struggling from somewhere within with emotions that he needed to both confront and to make known, but how to do this was the dominant question that plagued his subconscious mind at this moment in time. They watched Nuke and commented to each other how horrible he looks, and all from a simple fall with a barrel of nuclear waste that NEVER should have opened under any circumstances. The "Nuclear Regulations Board" assisted the "Department of Energy" throughout this whole case that most certainly perplexed and vexed all who were a part of it. Upon meeting with the victim, it was beyond clear to all of these officials, etc, that "Nuke" Wilcox was more than a victim; he was used, for some unknown reason, as a scapegoat for someone at the plant. Cellia and Jake Wilcox were now more than knowledgeable about just what is going to happen to Nuke, especially after talking to all of these professionals, but to actually hear first hand that they're only son is going to die, and how it will occur certainly served as nothing, but a way to break open the flood gates to a hellish domain

Mr. and Mrs. Wilcox talked a little with they're son, but he was very incoherent and could barely put two words together from what he had gone through. It was very hard for the couple not to look at the frightening equipment all around him that was being used to keep a hollow place in the body clear of run-off blood and infective bacteria as it "hissed" constantly. He was on his T.P.N. as well as fluids and I.V. antibiotics to save him from any possible infection. However he was still going to die nonetheless. However, the parents knew that when Nuke falls into his eventual coma, that the man will then pass away in peace and will not suffer any longer. They knew he was very, very sick from the radiation as it was literally "de-constructing" his bodily tissues, systems, etc, as it always does, but even now experts still do not know all there is to known about things as serious as this.

The manner in which Nuke's body is reacting is considered normal by professional standards, but it was inexcusable according to the parents of this poor victim now lying there directly before them. They were in the arduous process of losing they're son and, at least they know how he will die, but as for his time left remaining, that is solely up to the mind of God, which is the very one Nuke had always placed all of his trust in and has been abundantly recorded by all who meet this incredible, but pitiful man. He was indeed pitiful from what was being done to him as the byproduct of the radioactive waste, the radiation exposure at the plant, but through it all, Nuke Wilcox was a brave man who claimed a love of something deep inside of him that nothing could quell in the slightest. That something, is God, which Father Jason and other members of the Clergy here, knew upon first meeting this dying man. However Nuke was on occasion, saying things to his parents that made not much sense, like what he usually says, "Nuclear waste...nuclear waste...I'm nuclear....I was radioactive, Ha, ha, ha." He thought this statement that was in reference to him was funny, hence as to why he laughed all of the time while saying this brief self sentiment.

They held Nuke's paralyzed left hand that contained the inserted PICC line, and just stayed with him to somehow let Nuke know that they were here. His friends called him as well, and could equally hear that he was slowly, but surely fading away from them and all existence.

But his parents say that when they hear his voice, and hear his childlike laughter, they still know that he is there with them, and that makes them feel good…at least, for a while.

Nuke said to his parents upon leaving, 'I love you, and thanks for seeing me. Say Hi to my friends at the power plant." They always reply that they will, however, none of these two people who are his parents, will ever enter this place that took away everything form them, including form they're son who was talking after them right now. They knew better than Nuke, who was the victim of this incredulous place, that other than his truest friends, no one there really cares about him, except to take him to court, but this angered assumption was far from being of any truth. Rather, some people here, besides Nuke's longtime friends, were actually altering themselves and ways of thinking about what has happened and was so catastrophic as it was negligent and inexcusable, that there was really no tangible manner in which those who work there could actually not at least feel a flickering of concern or sorrow, directed the above mentioned feelings of empathy at this poor damaged man ; Mr. Foster for one.

At the "Sequoya" nuclear power plant Mr. Foster remained distanced from his previous endeavors as guilt now plagued this man of office in a very torturous manner. It kept him awake nights as the photos that had been revealed to him burned up and down his mind. He kept thinking back to why they had planted bogus files in the first place, as Nuke Wilcox was a loner, although he had friends here, but was considered as the bottom "rungs of the cooperate ladder." Normally this state of conceptual thinking about toxic waste workers does not manifest, but for some completely illogical reasoning it had here, and Nuke Wilcox was the brunt of their secretive motives and schemes. Nuke was considered as a subversive, because of the fact that he spent so much time by himself and preferred to work alone when applicable. No one should really be alone when dealing with dangerous and highly radioactive substances, whether they are isolated by lead suits, lead glass lined petitions or chambers, and using the robotics, etc, as well as handling the "plutonium #380," or any other type of manmade radioactive situation. However Nuke's safety was ill considered, because of this liking of his, and later people started to talk about this and decided he was someone who harbored a secretive plot to take over the plant and barter the plutonium to other "fellow terrorists" overseas; possibly the dreaded "Taliban." This was revealed in court and was considered as nothing short of rumors that bared no weight to them, as well as hollow lies and allegations about someone, because of the manner in which they prefer to work. The "Department of Energy" and the "Nuclear Regulations Board" investigated this immediately once the files had been discovered, and nevermind the area where the accident had happened. They though that the "Sequoya" power plant was trying to do what they profiled in the file of Nuke Wilcox and using him to throw investigators off the trail, like giving them something else to sniff so as not to bring attention to them, but no one could find the truth, and no matter how much these plant officials were cross examined by both sides, which included their own.

That's correct, nothing was found relative to this impossible fictional story plotted by individuals who had nothing to say, save for words of a rather diffused castigation.

After a brief time, which was during the week that Nuke had his stomach finally removed, Mr. Foster himself had made the arduous drive to finally see the victim personally, as he desired to truly talk with him, if applicable, and to make a formal apology, even of Nuke accepts it or not. It was something this man of high office had to do in order to not only clear his very repentive conscience, but to actually see what has truly happened to this poor man.

The finely dressed man walked into this place of appalling medical horrors, which had been formed by man's own creations, a manmade nuclear environment, etc, and held back his stringent emotions as they were immediately coming to the festering surface. He found a nurse who happened to be standing in the long hall and reading a patient's file. Mr. Foster introduced himself and quietly asked where "Nuke" Wilcox's room was located. She answered quietly that it was straight down the hall, and to count three rooms on his right. He humbly thanked her and went on his way. When Mr. Foster entered the room, but with ample caution in his heart and mind over what he will see, and stopped dead, but equally he made a fervent attempt not to have his sudden change of heart be noticed by this dying patient. However, Nuke had not seen this action as he was merely lying here and absorbing the peacefulness that was flourishing so amply within him. Mr. Foster said while approaching closer to the poor victim, "Hello, Nuke...you probably will not remember me, or even know who I am, but I'm Mr. Foster from the "Sequoya" nuclear power plant where you used to work." Nuke looked at this man who was well dressed and pressed, but who had a look upon his face that was extremely reflective of just what he has been secretly enduring as his eyes were now once again filling with tears. He took a seat next to Nuke's electric hospital bed surrounded with all kinds of medical equipment, which included the lavage machine, or suction, for his now removed stomach organ as the long tube was attached to a drain bag and the deviated side of this same tube went immediately into the machine itself. The "hissing" noise made by this equipment frightened the plant official, but right now he had not yet mentioned anything in pertinence to it. Nuke looked almost "gently" at Mr. Foster and softly spoke his extremely labored and painful sounding words to this man who obviously contained more courage than the rest of his fellow officials. Nuke said in his raspy voice, "Hi...ahhh. I'm nuclear." His mouth drooled a bit from the left side of his face being completely paralyzed, but he made seemingly good eye contact. His scrawny arms were held against his sunken chest that was getting steadily worse from the terrible radiation sickness that was obviously taking away his life.

Mr. Foster talked very kindly and humbly to this damaged man of gentle demeanor although he was dying because of their mistake. He said much to this poor soul lying here beside him, but again with words and a tone that was well benidictive of a festering and seething guilt that refused to subside. "How are you, Nuke? How are you feeling; are you in much pain?" ,asked the plant official caringly while looking at this man. Nuke turned his bald head in this man's direction and spoke to him, "I'm not in much pain.....(His voice slurred and was very labored and weak from what is happening to him.) I'm happy and they take good care of me. I like it here." He then groaned momentarily following his speaking; the bedding seemed to engulf his emaciated body, but in a comforting manner like a child in a bunting. The plant official suddenly remarked on the apparatus that he was obviously attached to as well as the "hissing" noise. He asked abruptly, because it's presence was scaring him, "Nuke, what IS that thing making the hissing?-It's terrible looking." He could not see beneath the bedding that he was attached to the machine and just how. Nuke replied in his drawn out, pained and slurred speech, "I…I have it for a week or so. I was operated on." "Operated on? What did they do to you?—I see scars all over your neck; they removed your thyroid, right?" ,Mr. Foster remarked candidly, but still very caringly. "Ughhhhh." ,replied Nuke tiredly. He was holding his paralyzed left arm closely to his side, but it rested atop the bedding, while the other arm was bent like the left, but he gently motioned it against the edge of the covers as if needing their presence for some reason that was completely an inward reflection or possibly some long repressed infantile emotions from long ago.

Mr. Foster spoke more professionally, but slowly to Nuke about his guilt as well as the fault of the power plant. He explained humbly, but earnestly, "You see, Nuke…What happened to you should never have been…The people who operated the robots that sealed and welded the barrels of nuclear waste didn't do their job correctly. I came here personally, as no one from the plant knows about us seeing each other today. No one…I came here on my own, because I wanted to explain to the best of my ability, that what happened to you was solely our fault, Nuke. I never went to the court sessions with your parents, so I had not seen the evidence or anything of the sort; only what little I had in the news and in the papers. Now when I finally see you today, well…I cannot believe the damage that has been done." Nuke responded to Mr. Foster, "It wasn't your fault…It was mine. The nuclear waste fell on me and got into my suit…no one else was to blame. It was just an accident…just an accident and I am nuclear. I was radioactive. Ha, ha, ha…radioactive." His face appeared like a brain damaged child as his smiled revealed the upper lip being more exposed than the lower. A gentle laughter emerged from this sensitive man who was so loving and equally forgiving, even unto the one who represents the place responsible for his traumatic and wrongful death that is soon to come. Something panged within the heart of Mr. Foster as he experienced this poor damaged man lying here next to him as he sat in a chair and will be able to eventually walk away form these death laden halls of this place where all patients come to die. Tears brimmed the official's staring eyes, but suddenly a nurse entered the room where they were talking as it was equally where Nuke lived. Her sudden presence startled Mr. Foster as he introduced himself as an official from the "Sequoya" nuclear power plant that has come to visit Nuke. She was Terry-Ann the nurse who literally loved this victim in a special manner and wanted to make certain he was protected, especially from individuals like these. She walked closer to them and spoke firmly to the visitor in Nuke's room. Terry-Ann asked, "Does Nuke know you?" "He does now, but before he hadn't; now look,…I understand you are watching out for Nuke's safety and I am sincerely gladdened at that, but I have come here only to help Nuke know and to understand that his accident was not his fault, but ours. I came here at my own free will and no one at the plant knows about this visit. I did not come here to cause malice or to harm this man. I was very sad when I finally saw photos of him from one of his friends, which turned out to be by an accident."

Nuke said suddenly, "He's nice….He tried to tell me it wasn't my fault, but it is. That's why I'm nuclear. I'm nuclear." His poor slurred and raspy voice sadly made itself heard amidst the momentary silence in his room; his home. Suddenly Mr. Foster asked the nurse, "Why does he say he's "nuclear?" Terry-Ann walked even closer to be physically near Nuke to give him a form of tacit and moral support while they spoke to each other, she replied to his reasonable question, "Nuke says he's "nuclear," because of the time when he absorbed over 500 R.E.M.'S of nuclear radiation, and his body was radioactive." "Oh, I see. That makes sense…That machine, what is that?" ,Mr. Foster asked her caringly. Terry-Ann explained it was a special machine that supplies continuous suction, because of his stomach being completely removed from a large tumor in it, as it completely blocked any passage of food from getting into the intestine, but the rest of his medical information was strictly prohibited from him knowing anything about it. Nuke replied amidst their speaking, "I was radioactive…radioactive, .nuclear. I'm nuclear."

It was so sad as it was heartbreaking to both see and to hear. The man was overcome completely with advanced radiation sickness that was causing his body to deteriorate, but Mr. Foster had no idea as to just what was happening slowly and insidiously to this man's body because of the raw nuclear waste spilling and from the massive exposure to this radiation, as the whole area had to be quarantined, and never mind the area surrounding this plant was to be evacuated manditorily. She finally left them alone once more to continue talking, but the nursing staff remain hidden in the distance of this place to make certain that this plant official was not up to any tricks that may cause him further harm. However this was not going to happen in any way, as Mr. Foster talked calmly and very humbly with this same man who was dying before him, as he was such a pathetic sight that caused this same man of power to remain deeply humiliated, because of not only how he looked and acted, but the personally acclaimed guilt that dwelled within him since gazing at these two photographs clutched in his hands as it was certainly the way of God in which this sudden turn of events were thusly manifesting into a reality. He sat there with this pathetic individual who was obviously clutching a flower of peace that so very few are capable of ever finding as well as cultivating.

Mr. Foster was so severely affected more so, because of finally seeing the man who worked so willingly and happily for years as a nuclear waste worker, and never once requested for another type of task. He just enjoyed being there and being an exclusive part of the work force, and nevermind doing something he loves, as well as what he had been solely and professionally trained for. When Nuke finally received his chance to work here, at the "Sequoya" nuclear plant, he was all a flutter like a kid in a candy store or when able to buy that special hard to find comic book that became out of print. Nuke's mind and heart, although was much of an adult, was still one who cherished the child within us all and used it to his daily advantage of it's assistance in knowing what truly matters in life and the rest of the universe, which is exclusively governed by our only God ;a living, breathing God who loves us to the point where He literally "handed over" His only begotten Son to die on a wretched cross for our sins and to destroy death forever. Yes, this is the flower Nuke Wilcox carries within him daily and throughout each night, as well as when the moment of his death finally comes, and soon. But just how soon?

Not even his physicians can truly tell this, because although his test results and his bodily status reflect unholy ending for him, it is the eternal living soul that dwells inside of this "husk" or "container," that will once again take hold of the "hollow of His mighty hand."
(Amen!)

Mr. Foster left the nuclear victim care facility a completely different man that day, as he never at all, in the slightest, expected in a million lifetimes to find a state of consciousness, and a literal loving form of forgiveness that is practically unheard of in this modern day that has become further and further depersonalized and computerized. Instead he found a severely damaged young man who was literally medically destroyed from this terrible and unspeakable industrial accident at their power plant, but he, the poor victim, lies there completely helpless, and does not grieve, nor does he swear vengeance upon this person who represents the place that had now "re-created" him and redirected his very fate, and moans peacefully a tacit "I forgive you, and your not to blame." Mr. Foster thought to himself, if that does not show people there is a true God in this world, then absolutely NOTHING will!

The following day Dr. Henkel walked into the room of Nuke to see how he was doing, and to see how much longer the man needs to remain attached to the lavage. He was in his blue scrubs and wearing a hat which is worn in the operating room, but goes tightly against the contours of the head. Dr. Henkel said to the poor man in a happy-go-lucky tone, "Hello there, Nuke. How are you feeling?" Nuke looked at the surgeon now standing there before him and replied with a twisted smile, which gave them the immediate knowledge that his brain functions were steadily declining. Nuke said in a happy form of return, "Hi. I'm good. Who are you?" (His memory was also declining considerably from the radiation poisoning.) "I'm Dr. Henkel, Nuke; the one who operated on you. I cam here to check on your cavity where the stomach was; remember now?" ,the kind doctor explain as he answered his valid question. "Yeah." ,answered Nuke tiredly, but comfortably. He went over to Nuke and gently spoke to the damaged man like one would to a child, but never once forgetting he is a grown man who was in a traumatic industrial accident and is dying as the result. Dr. Henkel spoke while gently removing the covers from his upper body, but taking care not to hurt his left arm containing the inserted PICC line as it delivered the continuous T.P.N. and the fluids in the other lumen. "Let's see what that looks like, all right?" ,Dr. Henkel smiled as he spoke gently to the poor soul who was very trusting as well as compliant to the surgeon's wishes, although he was having great difficulty in his comprehension. He had some trouble lifting the Johnny, so he mentioned to Nuke that he was going to run and get a nurse to assist while he inspects. Nuke patiently waited in silence as he looked down at something that was barely noticeable, but he could certainly see it was a tube extending form his emaciated body; the large suction machine immediately adjacent to him at his left. Suddenly the nurse entered the room as she accompanied Dr. Henkel. "And here we are." ,Dr. Henkel said gently. Nuke said, "Aaaahhhh." "I know, I know, Nuke. It's been a terrible road for you, but this will be over-this part of it anyway….I want you to try and remain as still as you can so the nurse and I can look. She's going to help me to hold the covers up while I inspect the site, okay Nuke?" ,the kindly surgeon asked this poor patient. Nuke did not respond, but he had with his bloodshot eyes and terribly sunken face. His left arm was gently moved out of harm's way while the nurse and the doctor motioned the bedding away from him momentarily. He immediately experienced coolness from not being beneath the covers, but still the poor man had not uttered a sound reflective of protest of any kind.

The nurse held the bedding up as Dr. Henkel pulled up his Johnny to see the site. "Oh, that looks good. I'm going to listen to you're space that is now empty, okay?" ,the doctor said. He gently, but firmly pressed the stethoscope against the now emptied area which once contained the stomach. The silent exam lasted for about five minutes, but then upon removing it from his ears and finally placing it over the back of his wide neck and allowing it to rest on his shoulders like a woman's night wrap, he explained to Nuke that everything sounds good, and that he will be back in surgery in three days to remove him from the machine. Nuke spoke happily and said to them, "The operating room? I like that room." "You like that room, do you?" ,the doctor asked with a smile and a bit of a chuckle in reply while replacing the bedding back over this poor patient. The nurse assisted as she smiled also in reply of his gently and innocent phrase. Nuke again spoke happily, "Yeah…I like it in there. It made me feel good and happy." "Oh, that was the all the drugs that we gave to you to make you sleep." ,Dr. Henkel explained, "The happy room, ha?" They all laughed together, as the nurse then cut in saying, "All of those happy drugs." "Ha, ha, ha, ha!!! That's right; the happy drugs." ,exclaimed Dr. Henkel happily while smiling at the both of them. On a more serious tone, the surgeon explained to Nuke that he will later be given a special oral diet, but he assured Nuke that he will never be removed from his intravenous feedings. He also told Nuke briefly about a special tube feeding formula, but could be taken orally, that is formulated for people who only have an inch of intestine and can absorb it, but not to worry, as this will all be discussed in a few days. Nuke was happy as he said, "Thank you for helping me." 'You're welcome, Nuke. We're glad to do it. You take care and you do what the nurses tell ya." ,the surgeon said kiddingly, which Nuke understood as he laughed like the nurse had. Dr. Henkel smiled at Nuke and tapped his left forearm and wished him well, but prior to leaving his room, he said, 'I'll see you again in three days." "Aaaahhhhh." ,Nuke replied in his extremely distanced and slurred voice that was very raspy as he was slowly losing his voice from the extensive damage from the radiation exposure.

Outside the room, Dr. Henkel talked further with the nurse about Nuke and how to care for him at this particular point in time. He told her to empty the old drain bag, as there was only an inch of old blood waste in it, as the bag had not been changed in three days. Dr. Henkel wanted to have a completely new one reattached to the drain tube so he could have it measured and to see if his diagnosis was accurate, because if it was not, Nuke would have to remain on the lavage machine for another couple of days after prognosed three days. He was well taken care of and later went into surgery to be surgically removed from the machine. This was done specifically to Nuke, due to the fact of his case being so bad and the fact that, because of the tremendous exposure to this nuclear radiation, his tissues and immunity will not respond to treatments accordingly as a normal patient will. Another series of flat X-rays were later to be carried out to check the status of Nuke's disintegrating intestines, which frightened the doctors tremendously. Fortunately his parents have already been told, but they also knew Nuke will have to be informed, but what to leave out?; and just what to tell him?

Chapter Nine

SOME TIME HAS LAPSED since Mr. Foster had come to personally visit the damaged man known only by his nickname; "Nuke." It was in the ninth month of his terrible acquired condition known as radiation sickness, and his brain functions have most definitely more than begun to diminish. Meaning his speech, as well noted, has become increasingly incoherent and more slurred, as well as his sense of competency if he has to make his own medical decisions, etc. Still the man was able to understand what was being said to him, but he was unable, most of the time, to truly give a response in return, save for either nothing, or his usual drawn out and very painful sounding moans in his raspy voice. His medical pain has grown further worsened as pain management assisted the victim, but unfortunately because of his tremendous list of drug allergies and interactions with other medicines he is now taking, especially for his lack of thyroid and the radiation sickness, which has changed his whole system entirely, there is not much they could do, but luckily his team of caring specialized physicians had come up with a better plan, as they were far more educated that the formers. But it was the man's tremendous inability to move as he is becoming more and more disabled from what has happened to him, as well as his body is finally succumbing indefinitely to the radiation sickness that is extremely advanced. To be truthful in the midst of this explanation, no one knows just how this poor man is remaining alive. His parents, Jake and Cellia Wilcox, have watched they're son deteriorate right before their eyes. This has caused them so much mental turmoil as well as a perpetuated anger directed at the "Sequoya" nuclear power plant which is solely responsible for everything. In fact, Nuke finally told his parents one day about the plant official, whose name he could not recall, had come to visit him and to apologize for the accident and it's gruesome affects. However, His parents were far form ebullient.

They were very angry, but his father was so angered by the otherwise "happy" news they're dying son had just given them that he had to get up from the chair and walk outside of the room for a while, but he then finally went into the family room, which was placed a good distance down the hall. Nuke asked his mother where he went, but his parent, loving and very gently with Nuke, replied that he is just sad and needs to go of by himself for a short time. Nuke, although was declining in the realm of his brain functions and awareness, etc, understood more than what his mother was telling him. Nuke, in his sad and mutilated voice that slurred so badly from radiation poisoning of this tremendous magnitude, said to his caring mother while she held his paralyzed left hand with the implanted PICC line, "I know Dad is mad at the plant… But I told them it wasn't their fault; it was mine. I…I'm radioactive…. The nuclear waste fell on me…Aaaahhhhh." He moaned in the last part of his broken statement directed at his mother who he had always loved very much, as even this ungodly affliction had not even begun to quell what truly lies within the heart of this damaged individual. Cellai told him, "It's all right, Honey. I know you believe the plant is not to blame, but you just stop worrying about that. We know what happened, Baby. Please rest now. Don't worry yourself about the plant anymore." She stroked the side of his bald head while looking over him in such a tender and caring manner that only a mother could do, as well as give the same effect that is seemingly eternal as it is surely a remnant of our Blessed Mother Mary; the mother of God.

Nuke still talked a lot, as nothing could yet stop this courageous man from attempting to reveal things that loiter inside. The nurses here took wonderful care of him, but things were indeed changing and not for the better. Nuke was now placed on continuous oxygen, but he already had been placed on a dose of six liters per minute, which is a hefty load. It had taken the man some time to get accustomed to wearing the nasal cannula, because it made his nose bleed and very, very sore. However after a month's time, he finally got used to it's rough presence and he stopped bleeding so much. Nuke asked them why he was placed on the oxygen, as he was no longer just burned and nearly dead from absorbing all of the nuclear radiation. They gently explained to Nuke that this is what happens when one is succumbing and dying form advanced radiation sickness, and they knew it was time to have someone explain it all to this poor man who was asking questions, and rightfully so.

A thanotologists, or death councilor, was assigned to talk with Nuke, but she was the same woman who has been working with him on occasion since his admission here nine months ago. Her name was Kathleen Gomez, and she was a well trained person who has worked here in this special facility for almost twelve years. In her reports, she wrote that she has never once met a victim like Nuke Wilcox, as he claimed to have a form of spiritual understanding that seemingly no one else in her reach has. However, Kathleen walked gingerly into the room of this sweet soul who was suffering so badly in his body, and probably in his mind, that even he had not known of it's relatively awesome presence.

Nuke smiled at her, as he had just finished watching television and placed the remote control down onto the table that was adjacent to his bed so he could easily reach things there. "Hi, Nuke. Remember me?" ,Kathleen asked in her sweet persuasive manner that was well representative of this dignified field. Nuke only smiled a rather hollow smile and replied that he hadn't. Kathleen sat down on a chair next to him as he looked at her contentfully and waiting for her to continue speaking for some unknown reasoning. He occasionally stared over at his two I.V.'s that were pumping seemingly forever into the dual lumens in his arm. The black burns had faded considerably, so his appearance had not looked so grim and loathsome to behold quite as it had when he first arrived. She introduced herself as a thanotologists, and explained what that was. Nuke understood without hesitation, which Kathleen was very gladdened at this fact that he still claimed some tangible brain function and connubiality. She asked Nuke if he knew what was going to happen to him before he dies. Nuke said that he knew he had radiation sickness, and that he was once "nuclear" from the exposure to literally hundreds of R.E.M.'s of said radiation. The caring and gentle woman sat here and talked to Nuke and told him if he does not want to hear anything she has to tell him, then to merely say that he doesn't want to listen anymore. He comprehended her rather exceptional compassion towards his unique fate, but not in here was it considered anything like that.

Kathleen told Nuke that eventually his brain that is still declining in functions, will eventually shut down and he will fall into a coma. Nuke's eyes widened themselves, but he asked gently, as if devoid of any realistic hardened emotion, especially from the prior damage encountered from the fall against the concrete flooring at the plant. Nuke asked her a battery of very valid questions, "Will you take care of me? Will I be washed and fed in my I.V.? What about when I get cold; will you get me warm? Will you help me?" His face was suddenly plastered with a mask of a silently perceived terror, but surprisingly it was not because of the coma itself, but what his questions so fiercely, but gently pointed themselves to-his care. She got herself closer to Nuke and said emphasisingly, "Oh course, Nuke. We will never stop taking care of you; we'll check your vital signs, we'll keep you warm, we'll make sure you keep getting your T.P.N. and we'll wash you and change your Foley bag—We'll do everything we are now, Honey. It's just you won't know it anymore." "What about my sugar-what if it gets low?" ,asked Nuke fearfully, but still in his labored voice that was slurred and drawn out in tremendous pain. "Of course, we'll check your sugar levels, Nuke. We won't allow anything to happen to you. You're going to be in the best of hands." ,Kathleen explained very passionately as well as calmly. Suddenly Nuke's face went back to being completely calmed and nonpossessive of any fears. Nuke asked her what a coma is like. Kathleen explained in her gentle ways, that it is like when he was put to sleep in the operating room when he had his stomach removed.

Nuke then smiled so peacefully as he looked at Kathleen, and in his slurred speech, he then said to her, 'Then when I die, I'll see beautiful things." With a tear brimming her eye following the man's words of a truth which he withheld in the firm clutches of certitude, she returned her comment and replied in agreement, 'That's right, Nuke...You will see beautiful things like God." Nuke suddenly smiled at her in a manner that he has never done before, and then the poor dying man said, "Yes, then I won't be nuclear...Aaahhhh." "That's right, Honey. You'll no longer have radiation sickness...no more "nuclear.," and you will be at peace." "I can't wait to die and to go home again...no more nuclear." ,Nuke expiated his witheld emotions, but at the same instant, he extended his right arm that was so emaciated as it was twisted and almost "gnarled" from being so affected, as he had approximately 38 blood transfusions since the accident, as his marrow continued to fail, but miraculously he did not have to receive a bone marrow transplant, although all are now saying he still should. Kathleen took hold of that shaking and jerky motioned right hand and felt the gentle soul emitting his truth that dwelled so permanently within him, but at the same time, letting her know of his very human need to grieve, but he was losing his ability for words, so Nuke merely rolled his head way back as he was now staring at the wall behind him where the head of the hospital bed leaned up against. Nuke then moaned for a few eternal minutes, but it was more than obvious here that the man was so fervently attempting to say how he truly feels, but again because of the tremendous damage to his brain from all of the radiation entering it during the accident, he was unable to find anything in his dwindled arsenal. He breathed heavily, but this was because Nuke was festering within, and Kathleen saw this happening. However She let go of Nuke's trembling hand and talked him out of it, but this was easily accomplished. He was filled with the acclaimed peace that has dwelled within him for so long, but the man was crying out, because he was upset about the coma which will loom upon him, but once more, it was not because of the condition, but rather the worry about his care. However he trusted this kind woman of a rare breed of compassion and human understanding that perpetuated itself in the lives of all of these poor patients in this facility for victims of all things "nuclear."

Kathleen eventually left his room, which was the man's home for the rest of his natural life. He had also been told earlier that he will not be able to breathe on his own as well as talk, but even this had not upset the man into any sort of festering psychological state like nearly all others following this kind of devastating information. Nuke didn't care about sliding into a short lived coma, because he knew, even in this state of declination, that he was not going to suffer, because he would be unconscious. He had been told by Kathleen that his parents were informed as well so there was no need for him to tell them, as well as to have the mentioned news of horror to upset him anymore than it already has. However through this unimaginable situation which has caused even the most professional minds in the facility to ponder, certainly did not want, for a second, to understand from a personal perspective what it feels like being told that one is going to fall into a coma prior to finally passing away. However Nuke had also been told that his intestines were disintegrating in a very real and literal sense of this frightening word. Nuke still could not be pushed away from the love in which his affection flows, which is God. He truly wants to die, and has been unconsciously readied since he was only a child, but this was something Nuke had expiated from the secretive annals within himself in journals at home, which at times were found by his mother. Nuke's eyes and his overall reactions in pertinence to talking about his condition and death, and just how it will come along, has caused nothing but the reinforcement of an indescribable peace that nothing can remove, as it was avidly viewed by all psychiatrists and thanotologists here, as well as his physicians. To put it as bluntly without offending, "Nuke Wilcox is truly benidictive of a Saint, but a Saint who's only destiny is to die away from radiation sickness."

The next day a meeting had taken place here in the alcove of the radiation victim care facility. The meeting consisted of a rather disturbing agenda that revolved specifically around "Nuke" Wilcox and the previous conversment about his eventual coma. Dr. Taft, the leading physician in this medical team who specifically cared for Nuke, had met with thanotologist Kathleen as she had to vent out her sincerest of inner concerns.

Amidst this conversation that was highly tense as it was relieving and calming, Kathleen vented out her feelings about this particular patient and his terminal condition. She spoke fluently about how she couldn't at all believe that this poor damaged man, so gentle in nature and personality, has succumbed to a relatively catastrophic illness because of the simple handling of barrels of nuclear waste from one place to another. While crying herself in the wavering realm of her words that certainly needed to be expelled forth, this same caring thanotologist mentioned to Dr. Taft that, "I just cannot believe that this man's very life has been destroyed from pushing a barrel of nuclear waste….(Pausing, she hugs a pillow in one of her long hands, while the other she temporarily cradles her mouth and chin amidst her poignant speech.)…"Nuke is our only patient who has lasted more than three months, and he could really talk—carry a tangible conversation with you." She was wavering in the realm of her emotions that were indeed the hardest she's so far ever had to face regarding these poor patients who come here from all over, but are always victims of nuclear accidents. Dr. Taft replied caringly and softly stated to this wonderful professional who has spent at least twelve years here amidst her profession of intense crisis and humanistic grief. He said in reply, "Kathleen, if handling Nuke's case if hard for you, then simply pass it on to someone else." "I can't, Dr. Taft." ,replied Kathleen very softly and emphatically. "Why, Kathleen? I see his particular situation is really tugging at you, and in a more hefty manner than the others you have dealt with here; how come, do you think?" ,Dr. Taft answered, but ended it with a tangible question. "Well, I mean…Look at him, doctor; Nuke is the only patient any of us have been able to really get to know, to talk with, and to understand what makes him "tick," and now we watch him literally fade away right before our eyes. And to tell him he's going to lapse into a coma prior to dying, ugh…." ,Kathleen's words ended with a controlled crying spasm as she professionally attempted to retain herself as a thanotologist, but as said, she really made a good and powerfully acclaimed point amidst her speaking to this particular doctor. She relinquished her sense of loyalty to this same physician regarding the needs of this poor man who has literally been destroyed and is rapidly dying from that terrible industrial accident that seemingly shook apart the American nuclear power industry, and nevermind his parents. It was obvious as it was clear that Kathleen had to pick herself up by the old bootstraps and continue her quest to assist a dying soul. Dr. Taft was certainly a friend in her predicament, but he was equally one when it comes to the personal needs of his colleagues. She was in a desperate tug-of-war within herself, but she refused the doctor's quest for her to simply pass the case to another colleague in her field and merely say it is due to either a conflict of interest, or the truth, "it's just too emotionally painful." However she declined, as Kathleen somehow felt she owed this damaged man something which he has been denied amidst his life as a critical, dying patient, and that was his dignity, and his hope for a good death, which Nuke had already made redundantly clear to not just her, but to everyone here at this facility. Yes, "Nuke" Wilcox was no ordinary patient.

Chapter Ten

THINGS IN THE MEDIA calmed down quite a bit since the happening some ten months ago, but there was still much controversy lying in wait to strike like a cobra coiled in readiness as it awaited for the opportune time to make it's terrifying presence known. The protesters who had come in droves to the "Sequoya" power plant in rural Tennessee, finally were driven away by authorities as they were making a scene and bothering the hundreds of employees as tensions became so heightened that many people who worked here became victim to ambushing and even physical attacks prior to passing through the gate. Many arrests were made and slogans of hate were silenced by mace carrying police trained for riots. People were terribly outraged at the "slap on the wrist" the plant received when the courts decided it's fate, but sadly the public had been misinformed about just what transpired on the inside. Although it was known publicly that the "Department of Energy" and the "Nuclear Regulations Board" had in fact taken the 'Sequoya" power plant to court and hired attorneys for the victim's family, it was not known that they are being watched on a daily basis and if they ever slip up once more, and regardless if it something that is minor, save for something that is definitely beyond anyone's control, the plant is either under further investigation or it is to be shut down indefinitely. But right now, amidst all of this upset and outrage that is being spread nationwide, this same victim lies her in the Tennessee nuclear victim care facility and waits to die. Nuke is in his eleventh month here and his brain function has greatly declined just as the team of highly trained physicians said would happen. Nuke cannot talk any longer, but he moans in his usual tone of a prolonged, raspy, and weak demeanor, as this is now the only way Nuke can commun9icate verbally. However, Nuke is conscious just the same, but for how much longer?

Nuke now weighs only 123 pounds, as he was 187 when he initially arrived. Receiving his T.P.N. , but h the PICC line had to be replaced, as it only retains it's use for about a year-sometimes a little longer. As he endured this literally often torturous procedure, Nuke cried and moaned the whole time, but the nurses and surgeon was very compassionate to this poor dying man whose body was rapidly succumbing to this severely advanced radiation sickness. Nuke couldn't stand the pain, but he did very well, as he had been unconscious during the prior time it was placed and had been done in an operating room, but with radiological capabilities like in certain hospitals, especially the large university hospitals. He was comforted accordingly, but Nuke responded with his smile that was so like this poor man as he was the talk of not only this place of medical care, but all over the state, as well as in national news. Nuke was rarely removed from his hospital bed as it went everywhere he went, which included in the operating room, as it waited for him next to the operating table, because he was so hard to move and to transfer. This time, in "angeo," where he received a new PICC line, they placed a litter board under him and lifted the frail and emaciated man of skin and bones, and lifted him back onto his bed as they made certain that his Foley bag was in no danger. Nuke smiled, because , to him, it was all exciting, but he certainly was glad the painful procedure was ended. Nuke gently reached for his new line, but this nonviolent act of curiosity was immediately seen and thwarted by the hands of a nurse. "No, no, Honey. This was just put in; it must be sterile. I know it hurts, but upstairs your nurses can give you more pain medication, all right? Don't touch it, Sweety." ,the nurse spoke tenderly to Nuke. The surgeon had already left the room, but the two nurses who assisted were here with him, while transport also had come by just in time to take him back to the "nuclear side" of the hospital. (This was the slang term all staff used for that particular part of the place, as it was not to be considered as derogatory or hurtful.) Nuke drooled while a nurse wiped it away. She wished Nuke good luck, and to be well, although she certainly understood that he was soon going to pass away. Nuke left his paralyzed left arm that received the new PICC line there where they left it, while his other arm, the right, he merely plucked gently at the nuclear symbol on the same side of his Johnny. Moaning gently and smiling, Nuke tried to "talk" with the rather young orderly, but the orderly had not known, so he merely smiled in return. A "contamination badge" was on the man's scrubs, which is a special badge worn that changes color that reflects how much radiation the wearer is absorbing, and if it turns red, then danger is stated by this color; the wearer is contaminated with radiation, but a dangerous amount and is in danger. Nuke was wheeled back to his room and everything was set up again, as he called in a nurse to assist him. Nuke drowsily watched them as he felt the pain from this procedure plague his arm in throbbing "glory" that is hard to beat, but is certainly nothing when compared and contrasted to his radiation sickness. He was 10 liters per minute by now, as his lungs were failing, or rather his ability to diffuse, or to diffuse oxygen through the capillary sacks in the lungs into the bloodstream, hence causing his heart to be taxed, which made him more weak and had more calorie burn, hence further alterations with his T.P.N. formula.

Nuke smiled and he was given an injection of Fantanyl through his PICC line, because a note had been sent up with him to let them know he was in a lot of pain. Nuke was happy as he moaned with his own personally acclaimed joy, which was his "joy of death."

Father Jason was always informed as he had been genuinely affected by this poor man's increasing afflictions which all sprung from this advanced radiation sickness. The priest was devastated after hearing that Nuke could now no longer speak, but only utter his usual drawn out raspy moans, but he was equally grateful that the same man could manage to still understand what was going on around him. In fact, it was he; Father Jason who was on duty that night when Nuke had been airlifted to the facility from the "Sequoya" nuclear power plant. After the many physicians and surgeons finished their work of desperation to save his remaining life, they called on this same priest to do whatever he must, which was to administer the sacred act of last rites. He told Nuke about this some months before, which the damaged man was happy, as he in turn abbreviated directly that this was probably the reason as to why he still lives. Father Jason was truly shaken by this simple man's wisdom that had been acquired from a literal lifetime spent in a unique form of isolation that was luckily intermittent, but certainly not permanent. The priest has worn these special lead lined suits before as he has been called many times to perform this sacred duty of our Lord God. However amidst all of the patients who come here to die; to never rise again and return to their jobs and to their families, etc, it was "Nuke" Wilcox who stood out above all the others here. This special young man had a soul like us all, but his sang out amidst the horrors of the nuclear age. His body was now badly ravaged and deformed from the simple act of falling with a large barrel of nuclear waste that contained an inaccurate weld, as even if this same man had not fallen with it, the tremendous nuclear radiation emanating from it, as no full shielding existed in this particular canister, was pouring out and bombarding the young man, although clad in a heavily lined lead suit used in these special applications. Radiation does not discriminate, as it reeked an indescribably and agonizing havoc within every area of this person's body. His intestines were continuing to literally disintegrate as this is the customary scenario in advanced radiation poisoning, which had been discovered that the waste Nuke had been carrying all of these years in the power plant, where it was not processed like in other plants before being transported to a safer location, contained a degree of plutonium, which is extremely high in nuclear radioactivity.

It was discovered by not only anatomical findings, but from pathological and phlebotomy findings, that Nuke's entire system was being broken down and where his brain had absorbed the brunt of the nuclear radiation, the damage was excessive as it was extensive, and often hard to decipher in many ways, but it was evident that everything displayed here was due to the radiation sickness which erupted from this accident at the "Sequoya" power plant.

His parents, Jake and Cellia Wilcox; were on the edge of lunacy as neither one could understand how and why he was still alive. All were saying that Nuke should have died during that accident as he was literally lying in a virtual "ocean" of raw and unprocessed nuclear waste. It was only the protection of his heavily lined suit of lead, which was very heavy and bulky, that had saved him this far. However it was the nuclear radiation which was more of the culprit. Now Nuke, although could no longer talk, was still pleasant as he was happy and very content in his world of unending pain and suffering. Nuke gestured that he needed something to drink by simply moving his capable right hand and gently tapping his mouth with the gnarled fist that has not been able to outstretch since this happened to him. He had done this same gesturing when he was in pain, or if he needed anything else, but when he wanted to talk, he could not, and one of the special nurses and even a counselor tried to help the man by giving him a pad of paper and a pen, but his hand was so weak as it was incapable of even holding onto anything, no matter how small, and his thoughts no longer were coming together in the form of sentences like a modern human being. Now, Nuke's brain relied specifically on simple gesturing and moans that varied in tone, which specified a particular emotion he wanted to depict at any given time. Pain was very easily noticed by everyone, especially in a place such as this. He slept more and more, which was one of the symptoms, but even long prior to that, Nuke happily anticipated this mode of mental consciousness we call sleep. He used to say it gave him peace from the pain, as well as was reminiscent of his faithful belief in the afterlife that nothing could ever shake from him. But speaking of his parents, Jake and Cellia came to visit the man more than usual, especially because it was being told to them that his life was rapidly declining. They sat near him and talked gently and tenderly, while holding the left paralyzed hand and arm that contained the PICC line. Nuke smiled like a child as he rotated his bald head that was healing some form all of the i.v. antibiotics, but what was noticed by them was the fact that Nuke's eyes, although have been bloodshot and very red since his arrival, have become blank and almost lifeless in nature. He rarely interacted with his eyes anymore as was explained to them, because his brain and consciousness was falling away, but probably into what is called as "mid-consciousness," which is a lot like being asleep, but the person is awake at the same time. They wondered if Nuke could be euthnaised, because his parents could not stand the suffering anymore, as the thought of him soon falling into the coma was driving the both of them into a state of near insanity. Unfortunately, this was absolutely forbidden, but they're wishes to have him removed from life supportive oxygen, NOT HIS T.P.N. AND FLUIDS, stopped if he supercedes the assumed length of the upcoming coma. They honored this, but the couple had been informed that he still may live, because he could still breathe on his own, as it is his lungs that are failing in reference to they're diffusion capabilities and the "gas exchange" factor, which is almost the same component of the lungs, but this is the ability of the lungs to be able to expiate, or to get rid of the carbon dioxide, the waste product of the lungs, combined with water and carbon, which rounds about 2% of water, and only 1% carbon. Still the Wilcox's were so much affected as they loved they're son with everything they had within them, but at the same instant, this couple wanted his suffering to end, although they did not want to say good-buy, but they know it has to be. Crying bitterly outside of the room containing they're sonly son, this couple testifies in a cloak of rage and embitterment over the nuclear power plant that spawned this poor man's "creation" and his "dereliction." However, Nuke still thought of that otherwise blessed "dereliction" of our Lord, Jesus the Christ, and His eternal promise to all who love Him and take solace in Him.

"For all who give me solace; I give the same unto you."   Amen
(From the "stations of the Cross")

The subject of nuclear waste kept emerging throughout the conversations of not only his parents, but from those who worked and were responsible for Nuke's overall care, but it had expressed itself more now that the man could not longer speak. However the parents of Nuke relayed to them very carefully that he had always carried a rather inert interest in the substance known as nuclear waste that was never considered to be anything problematic, but rather Nuke had always wanted to see it, and when he finally had at the power plant, it was like he found the "Holy grail." Nuke, for some odd reasoning that was his own, withheld a childlike fascination about it. Now his fascination with this substance has caused him to literally wither away and die. Nuke was becoming more and more incapacitated from this nuclear waste, but as said more so form the radiation levels that were lethal to all living matter, which much included Mr. "Nuke" Wilcox.

Jake and his wife shared much of they're innermost feelings about this, but not much had been exploited by the news media. However the officials at the "Sequoya" nuclear power plant made a genuine and even courageous attempt to make a formal apology in writing to the Wilcox family, but it was done through the mail. Unfortunately the Wilcox's refused the plant's apology, as Jake had written them back with a poisoned pen, and told them blatantly, "You can apologize all you want, but that will not get our son's life back. I will have you shut down if it's the last thing we ever do!!!....Go and see our son now, and see the man who you thought as nothing, because he hauled away you're filthy waste; the very waste that has given him advanced radiation sickness.... We hope you die!!!" Fortunately this reply was not considered an a threat or as anything to get the authorities involved, but regardless of this tragic circumstance, the "Sequoya" power plant sill occasionally attempted to make it's feelings known.

Nuke's needs have begun to load up, and the staff still took compassionate care of this victim. Nuke was genuinely "loved" by all who worked in this specific are of the large medical facility as he has touched the hearts of all who came into contact with him. His friends still occasionally visited him to attempt to bring the poor soul back to his original personality, but others were not living in delusionment in pertinence to the man's terminal state. They all stayed beside this poor man who knew them, but could not respond in a verbal manner. However despite eyes which reflected the looming and vigilant presence of death, Nuke still smiled at them as he recalled the "good times' at the power plant. He tried to mouth the words "nuclear waste," but sadly he could not be understood. He was a dreadful case as no one in all the world could in the least bit comprehend as to just how he was living after all this time, and it was now thirteen months since the accident at the plant. His friends couldn't forget how the entire plant had to be shut down in regards to cordoning off the area that was contaminated with excessive and highly lethal radiation as alarms went off everywhere and the tremendously vociferous tone of them as they screamed out danger all over the plant. When it had been found that it was Nuke who had fallen with the barrel and it had opened and spilt the contents, which was the highly radioactive waste, no one could believe it, as they all knew too well that his life had finished, but here he is now in front of them. It was an impossibility, but Nuke was still here with them. But how?!

In the meantime, Nuke's condition had paved the way for further recognition of laws that protect the general and overall safety of working conditions at all national nuclear power plants, but the parents of this poor victim stand by his side who's presence is languishing as he grows steadily weaker and weaker. However Nuke's smile distinguishes the fact that he knows who they are as he occasionally moans and smiles or stares at those who are nearest to him. He now weighs only 119 pounds, and has received three more blood transfusions as his marrow is getting set to fail once again. This unending spiral of agony and suffering that is experienced by Nuke is most certainly seen as it is understood, but only from a view that is rather detached. Nuke gently reaches out his right hand to his parents as this surely is his way of telling them a bunch of things, like firstly that he loves them, and lastly, to say his "good-bye." A friend who has meant the most to Nuke brought in for him, his radiation contamination badge that he wore every day while working at the plant, as he pinned it directly to his chest, but especially to his lead lined suit that was so very bulky when moving these dreaded barrels of raw unprocessed nuclear waste. He pinned it to Nuke's Johnny, and as this act of love was carried out, Nuke smiled in remembrance of all of those time he had—his life after college—the "Sequoya" nuclear power plant in Tennessee. Nuke gently touched it at his right chest, which was near the patch on the Johnny which told staff that he was a radiation care patient. He tapped it and smiled as he never wanted to close his eyes, because to this poor damaged man, the contamination badge was just it; a badge of his personal honor which well signified to himself and to his other family, that he made something of himself that was worthwhile and very important, as there could be no power plants which run on nuclear power without people like Mr. "Nuke" Wilcox.

His parents came to see the man more often as earlier said, but for some odd reason, it was Jake, not Cellia, who appeared to be taking things much harder than his wife although she too was extremely angstrous. This poor mad moaned out his raspy and deepening voice that was just what it sounded like; a moan. Cellia sat closely to Nuke and stroked the top of his bald head, as he could not have his face touched after all this passing time. He just turned the age of forty-two as it was surely a miracle that he was able to even be aware of this, and nevermind the undeniable fact that he was alive and conscious; but for how long?

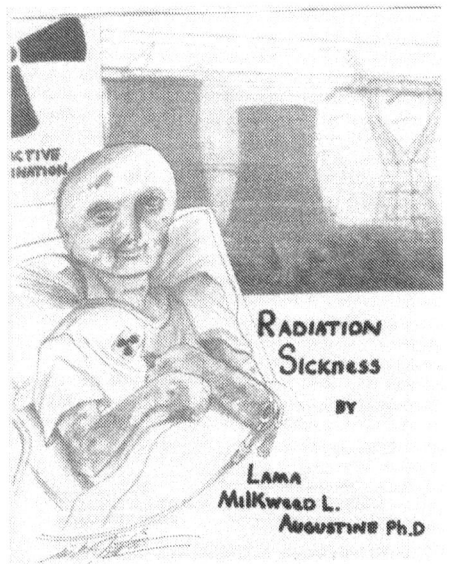

"This is "Nuke" Wilcox and his father, Jake in the radiation care facility in Tennessee on the night of the spill. He is in quarantine, due to being highly radioactive from his body absorbing literally hundreds of R.E.M.'S of nuclear radiation, which no one thought this man could live in all reality, but somehow he had. At least, for the moment."

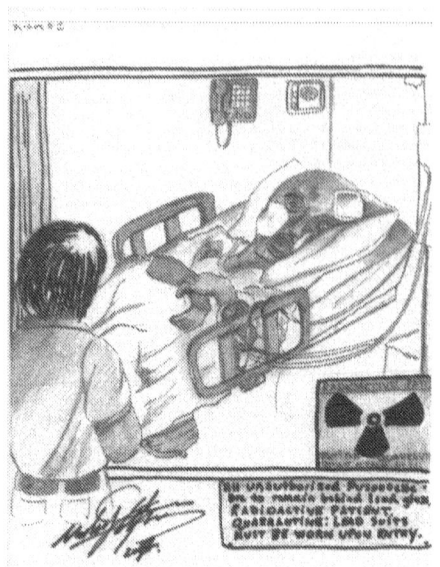

"Nuke" Wilcox some months following the terrible industrial accident. His situation is grim despite his contentment and full understanding of the fact that he has severe and advanced radiation sickness and is soon going to die. It had been only five months since this happened at the power plant."

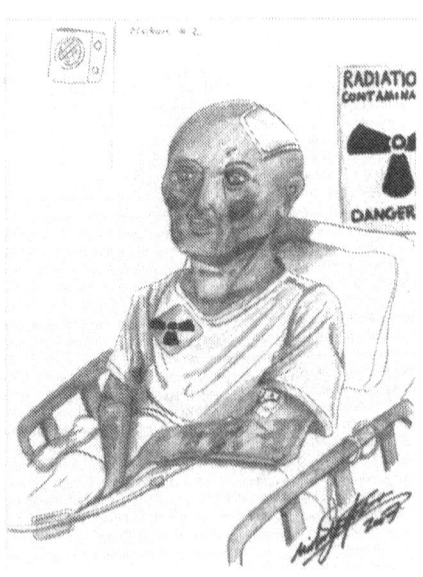

"This is Nuke with his parents, Jake and Cellia Wilcox. The man who is they're son lies before them as he is rapidly declining as his body is deteriorating from the radiation sickness. Already at nine months, he can barely speak and is losing this ability as said what will happen, and has lost a tremendous amount of weight despite his intravenous feeding since his arrival. The man peacefully anticipates his death that is all due to the negligence of the nuclear power plant, but still, even in this unspeakable medical state this damaged man is in from it, he still refuses to despair and believe it was the plant's fault."

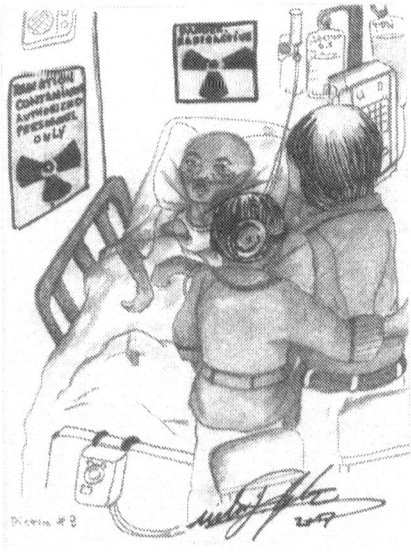

"Nuke" at the "Sequoya" nuclear power plant doing what he loves; being a toxic waste worker, which was what he had done since his arrival at the plant twenty-one years ago at the age of twenty. He loved working with the nuclear waste, and was very responsible and careful. Notice the contamination badge at his left cheat, as it becomes red when dangerous levels are about. Again, falling with the one defective barrel with the badly done weld, but this still made no difference as the lethality of the nuclear radiation coming from it was what had done him in for good. Now because of his love for all things nuclear, this poor man lies in wait and will slip into a brief coma before finally dying from advanced radiation sickness….How sad, and how tragic."

Chapter Eleven

THINGS WERE GETTING HIGHLY emotional both here at the nuclear patient care facility and at the Wilcox home. His parents, who loved him so very much, could no longer bare the strain that had been so suddenly thrust upon them that very bad day when they received a telephone call from the nuclear power plant telling them they're only son was in a lethal industrial accident. The terrible fate that they have seen and experienced along side him, as they too felt as if they were lying there in the bed beside him and going through all that he was, and nevermind will be. Jake personally remembers Nuke as a little boy who had always loved all things nuclear, but again, his fascination was a healthy one. By the time Nuke aged three years old, he always told his mother and father that he was going to work at the "Sequoya" power plant that was located only two miles away from where they lived. He pointed excitedly at the plant that was in the distance on this newly constructed highway and says how much he loved that place, and that he wanted to work there more than anything in the world. Nuke wanted so much to be a part of something great; of something of great worth to his fellow man. Unknowingly a child's innocence can follow him when that person finally grows up and no longer thinks of childish things, but it was because of that imperishable childlike innocence just noted, that was the eventual culprit in determining Nuke's very life, and now his very death. The excruciating mental anguish that is daily expressed between this loving couple, as they stare at many color framed photographs of they're bright and brave son while he was in college, dressed in his lead suit at the "Sequoya" power plant, but it was a professional studio shot, as his smile was reflective of pride and a powerful inner sense of achievement, which he thought like his parents, nothing can steal away. However it was also the older photographs of Nuke as a child growing up, as he wanted his mother to take his picture on the side of the highway standing there with the same power plant behind him. He was only the age of seven when the initial one was taken, as his little smile was bright and shiny, like the true innocent child he really was, as he was equally so full of a perpetuated hope that seemingly couldn't break it's fierce grip, but it finally had. All good things must come to an end, so they say, and how awesomely true.

Nuke was now into his fourteenth month here at the care facility and he was becoming less and less mentally aferbile and conscious, but he was mildly aware of things around him, as well as what people were saying. He was experiencing terrible pain, which lasted for approximately nine days before nurses realized what was going on, as this was because he barely moaned anymore, as the task was becoming increasingly difficult because of his total lung capacity was surely fading. Although his Fentanyl was daily given, it had not touched this particular pain. A doctor was called in who was a specific part of the team caring for the victim. He, with a nurse present, checked out Nuke, as it had been earlier noticed that his complete lower abdomen was distended and he was very ill. The doctor listened to it and heard sounds that were reflective of a very upset gastric tract, but he wanted a complete series of X-rays taken of his bowel and perhaps something could be seen that may be the culprit of this relatively new condition.

They were done, as all remembered him, and felt so badly for this prolonged suffering of the nuclear victim who had again come to them. Nuke wore his radiation contamination badge that had been given to him by a friend from the plant, as said, but the nurses pinned it back onto each Johnny as they changed them every two days. It was a regular film badge as noted, with a large circle in it's center, but sort of radiated out across the whole length of the rectangle shaped piece of protection, or rather alarm for the wearer. This served as an incredible psychological comfort to the damaged man, as it represented what he had done as well as the plant itself, as well as his many friends who certainly loved him. He smiled at it constantly as his profoundly weak right hand would reach out for it as it was pinned to his right atop the nuclear symbol patched onto these particular johnnies as mentioned. Moaning in a contented form of peace that only Nuke himself would be able to fully comprehend, this radiation contamination badge that he loved in a profound way, kept him probably more accepting that he would otherwise be without it. Tears often were seen rolling from the withered eyes of this poor wasted soul being savagely destroyed from hundreds of R.E.M.'S of nuclear radiation as he looked at it and even tried to temporarily hold it, although the object was pinned securely to his Johnny. He mouthed the words, "The plant." A nurse who cared for all of these poor people here, saw this silent form of communication that most of her colleagues missed, which was another reason why Nuke was caught crying. She caressed the top of Nuke's bald head and spoke tenderly to him about the power plant and the badge he was wearing. She knew about it's presence, because of it being mentioned copiously in his files, as well as hearing it from other fellow nurses here. Nuke smiled through a cloudy haze of warm tears which had come from his sorrowful soul, although it was still cradled exclusively in the bed of eternal peace and sleep. Nuke mouth to her, "NUCLEAR... NUCLEAR...NUCLEAR." Tears sat in her eyes as well. She gently kissed the top of Nuke's bald head and said in a sweet form of reply, "I know, Nuke. I know you WERE nuclear; you were radioactive." Nuke heard the word "radioactive," and smiled while motioning his head back so it faced the wall behind his bed. He tried so hard to laugh, but he contained not the capacity to do this task most of us take for granted.

She smiled at this poor patient in return as pangs of deep pity emerged from her, as she just recalled amidst this rather sweet moment, that another patient died this morning further down the hall. She told Nuke that she has to leave the room as there are more things to do, but to ring the call button if he could, but it was unanimously known that Nuke was no longer capable of doing this, so he was checked on continuously whenever possible.

The afternoon of this same day, the X-rays came up to the radiation victim care facility so his doctors could inspect the films of the complete lower gastric tract. The surgeon Dr. Henkel was also there to assist in deciphering. They were talking professionally about what was seen on these films, which so far, revealed that he had some stool lodged in the terminal ileum, or small intestine, and terminal meant the end stage of the said section of bowel. However upon further inspection, Dr. Henkel saw just below the place where he removed Nuke's stomach, a large blackened mass or spot on what would be his left side of the intestine. A form of silent panic interrupted these two doctors as they equally noticed what was already known would happen in cases of severe advanced radiation sickness from nuclear substances or environments. Meaning his entire bowel was thinning, or rather the walls were literally thinning so much, that in some places it was easily seen that perforation was upcoming, and he would die a horrific death.

Dr. Henkel and Dr. Pierce, another physician on Nuke's care team, but was also a Professor on the medical effects of excessive nuclear radiation exposure on human tissues and vital organs, and had spent over twenty-eight years highly involved in a die hard, tongue-in-cheek-research, certainly saw that this spot in Nuke's intestine was cancer, but not a regular form that is customary to the masses, but rather is more generalized to those in the nuclear industry like those who work in nuclear power plants such as 'Nuke" Wilcox. They measured the dimensions of the rather large spot on the film, as they were done right to actual size of the victim's body, hence measurements could be made accurately. Dr. Pierce and Dr. Henkel measured the black spot as being in width, 1 1.4 inches, and the length was approximately 3 4.7 inches, antero laterally measured 2 1.3 inches, while distally it was completely flat and level with the intestinal wall. Suddenly an overall feeling of great and steadily deepening sorrow filled this small, but spacious room. The X-rays were being sadly removed from the lighted wall while it was Dr. Pierce who said on his way out, "Now I have to make a phone call.... Thanks, Phil" Dr. Pierce walked from out of the X-ray examination room and said aloud to himself disgustedly, but sadly just the same, "Oh, shit. (sigh)"

Dr. Pierce called the house of the Wilcox's but found only Mrs. Cellia Wilcox. She was immediately thinking that her son had just died and she began to cry unrelentingly, but the caring man of medicine calmed her down and explained that this wasn't the reason as to why he was calling her. She had a wall mounted phone, so she merely sat there in a chair in the kitchen while the television was running softly in the distance. She listened very emphatically to the words of this Professor and physician for all nuclear victims and was a powerful promoter for their rights as well as ethical treatment and care; from every part of the person. She was crying softly while hearing the words spoken very carefully to this tear struck woman who was still in the unholy and drawn out process of losing her loving son-her child, although fully grown and a man, but a man who worked for twenty-one years at a well known nuclear power plant and handled deadly nuclear waste, and all because he loved anything nuclear. As she was writing down things while the physician talked with her about their discoveries. Tears rolled from her eyes no longer, because she just somehow realized that in order to record what she heard correctly, she must not be overwhelmed with tears and crippling emotions. However when the conversation had finally ended, she hung up the wall mounted phone and cried face down on their bed with the words she recorded in her hand. As if she had not desired to let go of what was heard, but this wasn't at all the case, but rather she merely forgot it was in her hand. They're world was crashing down all around them since the day arrived when he went off to work and fall with the barrel. But just think of how Nuke feels!!!

Yes, Nuke's body was still in it's process of disintegrating as the effects of the extremely highly and lethal levels of nuclear radiation had thoroughly done it's work although the time at the plant has surely long passed. But Nuke was sleeping more and more as priorly noted, and he was losing interest in his television which he liked and needed for company when his parents weren't there, because otherwise it was the nursing staff and his team of physicians who became his new "family," as this nuclear patient care facility became his "Home" for the remainder of his natural life. Because of the "Department of Energy" and the "Nuclear Regulations Board," Nuke Wilcox who was the victim of this power plant, made it absolutely certain that it would share the payments each month for the man to remain here and worked it out with his insurance company, as this was considered a rare case in the nuclear accident issue, because most people who succumb to these kinds of nuclear/industrial accidents do not live nearly this long, and nevermind are able to leave the place where they have originally been to receive their care, etc, and to return home, yet are able to receive home nursing, critical home care, etc. However not Nuke. This was because, he was surely going to die and there was not a damn thing anyone could do about it, and not putting aside the terrible and even frightening fact that he was literally radioactive for a period that lapsed well into seven weeks and was in strict quarantine, or what is known as "RADIOACTIVE PATIENT QUARENTINE…" Nuke was not told anything further about his worsening condition, but even more so because of his lack of comprehension, and the furthering news would only upset him as it was not at all considered as anything healthy from a psychological perspective to reveal things as this to a tragically or catastrophically ill and actively dying patient.

Nuke was kept very comfortable and his T.P.N. formula was not altered anymore, save if something went down too far, as he was still wasting and losing more and more weight as he now weighs only 101 pounds! There was not too much skin, surprisingly, which comes from a person losing an excessive amount of weight, but this man did not have it. Rather because of the terrible affects of the highly nuclear radiation, his poor body was withering away to literally nothing and he was steadily deteriorating into a living, barely breathing corpse as his skin was dry and his eyes, still exceedingly red and eternally bloodshot since the accident, stared contentfully through a graying skin that was becoming more and more devoid of life, as he appeared like he emerged from the very barrel that re-created him and this appalling, yet tragically sad condition as a "nuclear victim." Nuke was once a strong capable young man filled with the simplistic love of life and family, as well as all that really mattered to him. His left arm, the one that contains the inserted PICC line, was completely paralyzed, and the other arm, the right, still at times managed to touch the radiation contamination badge that was given to him in remembrance from a very dear friend at the power plant so he would be happy and never forget them, as well as the place of work he loves. There are no windows here in this area of the special hospital or facility, because of the radiation factor as professionals carrying geigercounters checking for background radiation, walk up and down these semi-darkened hallways. They wear lead lined white suits like Nuke had, but theirs were not as heavy as his, because they were not handling nuclear waste and working in a nuclear power plant.

But, these workers wear them to protect themselves from the same thing that sent Nuke here in the first place-nuclear radiation-which they even wear while they enter the rooms of these patients for a temporary moment to unlock the sharps box that is on every wall, and place a new empty one inside of the locked container mounted to the wall. Nuke sees this and he merely smiles and sometimes thinks he is back at the "Sequoya" power plant and is going to return home at the end of a long, hard work day, but no; this is all a hallucination as it was fueled by what he sometimes sees like that spectacle just described. He had not known it, but this morning another man just died down the other end of the hall as barely anyone remains here at this moment. The place houses at least seventy beds, and now there is less that forty as they have all died away and luckily there are no more victims coming. But what of poor "Nuke"? How much longer does he have to wait to leave here? His suffering that was so intensive had recently been quelled a great deal by the tender and loving efforts of the medical staff. He had lost eighty-two pounds in fifteen months, but is soon to lose more and more. His picture was taken from a friend at the power plant and sent to a local paper, which was immediately published so all could se this terrible and equally tragic; apocalyptic horror that writers were calling out right, "...An abomination of official ethics in the secretive workings of our nuclear power plants....'Nuke" Wilcox; the victim of the "Sequoya" nuclear waste spill has surely set the stage for these poor wretched souls of industrial accidents to be further protected....laws have been changed to protect "us" civilians from harm, but what about those who work in these nuclear power plants?-HEAR THEIR OUTCRY! What of the families of these same people? How do they receive compensation for these outrageous deaths brought onto them from the highly infantile foolishness and negligence of heavy industry?.....HERE, HERE for the Tennessee "Department of Energy!"

Photo taken by Roger Valentine, friend of victim

As earlier said, the parents of this poor wasted man who once was they're only son, lies on his hospital bed and calmly awaits his common fate that binds us all as one; death. The weeks crawl by and the physicians are on edge as if waiting for the rhetorical bomb to drop, but in the meantime, it is the parents of Nuke Wilcox who keep coming to see they're child, and to perhaps see something quivering in his now blank stare, but on occasion, he gives them mere glimpses of the glorious reality that he had always thoroughly acknowledged since the earliest of childhood. Jake and Cellia Wilcox are seated not in his room at the moment, but were in the family room with the door closed with Kathleen, the thanotologist who has been dealing specifically with the case of they're son. In her tender and calming manner that is highly reflective of this humble field, she comforts the couple as a fervency of love that is highly experienced for the damaged man lying in a room here down the long hall unknowingly awaits for their company.

Cellia cries and her husband comforts as they are seated together on the rather small couch there in the encasement of the family room Cellia explains through her crying, that she just can no longer take seeing they're son like this, as he is wasting away from the radiation sickness, while her head now lulls itself into the chest of Jake, her husband. Jake folds his right arm around her, which is the one closest to her, and tells her, "I know, Baby...It will be over soon, and his suffering will not be anymore." Kathleen cut in gently and said to them, "Yes, Nuke is really a sinking ship...there is absolutely nothing the doctors could ever hope to do in this kind of a situation, Mrs. Wilcox. I know this is going to sound very cold, but this is the correct time when you must learn to tell yourself that it's time to say good-bye. You have to let him go--." She cried more after hearing Kathleen's unbiased words of truthfulness and is one who surely emanates a very realistic form of caring for these particular people before her. She was momentarily cut off by Jake, but he was speaking only to his wife clutching his cheat. Jake said softly, but with a quivering lip, "Yes, Cellia....That man lying there is no longer our "Nuke"; he's a shell devoid of life, and he doesn't know us anymore." "That's correct, Mr Wilcox ." ,interrupted Kathleen as she suddenly bent herself forward with her hands folded to help and make better eye contact. Cellia suddenly said, "No, my son is still alive; so that makes him a man. How dare you say something like this in front of me and my husband. This is blasphemous and I won't hear another devilish word coming from either one of you." She abruptly grabbed hold of her old purse and jumped up from the couch, away from her husband's once caring form of acknowledgement and outreach, and left the room. "Cellia!-I'm sorry, Kathleen. She has never acted like this." ,Jake commented fervently and emphatically while jumping up to retrieve his severely distraught wife. "That's all right, Mr. Wilcox. This is very common as she is grieving and she is facing her son's immanent death, but I believe because it was brought on from negligence and lack of the care for his safety, this is what is making things much harder for her to bare....Just be patient, Mr. Wilcox, and she will allow herself to grieve openly-it will come, as most people do not being to grieve until sometime after the death of a loved one or a friend. Just watch out for her, as I can see a time bomb getting set to detonate, because of the fact this is a "wrongful death" here. She needs you're support." This kindly and very knowledgeable woman expressed her truthful observances here in this very sad and unfortunate situation. Jake thanked Kathleen in an appreciative and sincere manner, but he went out the door in search of his wife who is so full of intense spiritual and psychological grief.

Jake found her holding the paralyzed hand containing the PICC line in her hands as she was trying to warm it up by the mere heat of her body. Tears rolled from her eyes as she thought extensively about what the power plant has done, and how the affects of this nuclear radiation killed him, but in a rather slow and insidious degree of tremendous deterioration that is unlike anything she has even seen or heard of, save from the famed segments from the bombing at "Iro-Jima" in Japan, and all of those people had died immediately as they were at ground zero when the atomic bomb hit. She was wavering in a stormy ocean of a burning and silent fury, but it all was solely directed at the "Sequoya" nuclear power plant where he worked so happily and proudly for a period of twenty-one years. Yes, Nuke gave these precious years of his young life to the nuclear industry, because of a strange kind of love he carried within. She was now recalling, at that moment, his room at home, as it has not been touched , but only to keep clean; like a shrine in praise of they're brave and God fearing son who they loved indefinitely and with truly unconditional love' like the four wonderfully done models of nuclear power plants he had made as a young teen as they were put together with such precision and accuracy, and "love."

Jake found her and he wrapped his hands around his shaken wife. She immediately responded and apologized to her mate, but Jake told her to just forget about it and her reactions were not to be felt ashamed of. Nuke slowly turned his bald head at them and smiled, but it was not really considered as one with emotion, but rather as a reaction supplied by the stimuli that was there beside him. Nuke's severely shriveled face was dry and looked like he had been exposed to something highly radioactive, which is that very characteristic look that when one sees it, one never forgets it. He moaned out, but it was scarcely above a whisper. His bloodshot eyes stared intentfully at his parents although Nuke had no longer recognized them, but there was obviously something loitering there deep inside of the man that caused him to smile, because he never does at anyone else since this furthered state of deterioration had become this advanced. They both looked intently at the withered face of they're only son very closely and saw him mouth something that was completely legible to the both of them, "I love you." With that same mouthed sentence so brief, it was also heard that a sound emerged from him, and it was a gentle and very conscious groan of pain, but reminiscent of joy. Before leaving, Cellia had taken her left hand and stroked the top and edges of his bald head and kissed him affectionately several times in the same place. Cellia, his mother, said softly and with an undying affection, 'Good-buy, my nuclear…I love you, Baby…My Nuke. Good-bye, we'll see you again, and again." She then kissed him once again atop his bald head in a tender and loving form of affection. Tears fell from the eyes of her mate who was standing behind her, but he had quickly wiped them away. She moved aside so Jake could do the same, and he did. Jake, his father, said softly, but in a manner that had not been as drawn out as his wife, "Good-buy, Nuke.…We'll see you again soon. (Jake kisses the top of his bald head tenderly twice.) We love you, Nuke." They look at him once more prior to leaving him alone in the room at this special care facility for nuclear patients. (Radiation Care Facility) With they're hand- in- hand manner of walking, they turned and again said "good-bye," then departed from the room. Nuke was silent as all that was heard was the oxygen, as he was up to fifteen liters per minute, and it was now easily approximated that Nuke had less that a month to live, as it has so far been a total of seventeen months this man has lived here, and very comfortably, save for the pain that was afflicted from not only the radiation sickness, but from surgeries and the act of deteriorating and dying a very painful death, which again was all from being exposed to that lethal does of nuclear radiation. But to Nuke, it was all an accident; yes, all an accident, and there was certainly nothing at all to be the cause for blaming the "Sequoya" power plant for his mistake-according to Nuke Wilcox.

Chapter Twelve

"NUKE" WILCOX AS HE is now barely conscious. He is very soon to fall into the coma that was explained would happen just prior to his horrific death. He has lived with an undying form of humility that was found in living day to day with a profound belief in God and His Heavenly Kingdom. His parents are in the fierce clutches of terrible grief as they see that this is all from the "Sequoya" nuclear power plant as he had given to them, twenty-one of his precious years happily, but now with the advanced radiation sickness, and the nuclear waste literally coming into contact with his body as it leeched through his heavily lined lead suit used for this specific task of handling nuclear waste, had equally caused apocalyptic damage to the body of this poor damaged man. However, he still knows his parents; an impossibility? No, especially where the living soul is concerned, and when that same soul clings to God, all things are surely possible and very real.

Nuke is soon going to die, and will find his peace which he firmly believes exists."

Nuke still eludes the coma that presides over him and holds him firmly in it's untimely clutches, but the nurses, doctors, and the Catholic Clergy, come to him and tenderly administer care, and the offerings characteristic of the God who so loves us. At the very same time, and at a long distance of one-hundred and fifty or more miles away, the "Sequoya" nuclear power plant stands here majestically amongst the beauty and luscious fields of this area of Tennessee, as it was the very place that is the undeniable cause of this poor man's present situational condition. Peace fills his mind that is very mildly conscious, but he cannot speak, move or do anything else, however, he can still think on occasion, and he thinks of his parents, his friends at the plant, the moment of when he fell with the badly welded barrel of nuclear waste, and all of the good and highly compassionate people who cared for him. Seeing the numerous metal signs all over the walls of his room made him smile as he often thought he was still working at the nuclear power plant. Nuke occasionally caressed the radiation contamination badge on his right chest that was faithfully pinned onto each of the new johnnies by the nurses. The light was turned off all of the time now here in the sanctity of this room, because Nuke could no longer appreciate the television or anything further, but in all actualness, he could, yet Nuke could not even begin to tell this truthful fact to anyone here, so Nuke merely lays here daily and nightly waiting for someone to simply turn on the television, but it never comes. The light only turns on by the nurses or those from the lab, or his doctors, pulmonary therapists, etc, and once their reason for being in here in finished, they turn the light back off and leave him in the dark, but the dark insulated green curtain that covers the wide window in each of these patients' rooms, allowed some light to filter through, but the nights here were not like in a regular medical hospital setting, as the overhead lights are dimmed down to almost nothing at 10:00, while there are other times when there is no light at all. Nuke finally accepted this otherwise sad and upsetting situation, but he appreciated the continuous care that was still going strong. He thought a lot about his radiation sickness and how it has made him this way; a sad, a highly pitiful sight that is very soon going to pass away. Nuke was finally down to 93 pounds, but he will probably no longer lose any more weight, and regardless of the fat emulsion that is heightened and occasionally lowered in this formula for his T.P.N. it has been avidly discovered that because of his bowels' rapid thinking and their cancerous legion, although flat, was responsible for the man's intensifying malabsorption and wasting.

In another two weeks Jake and Cellia Wilcox were together at home, as Jake had a few days off from the foundry. Cellia was in the dinning room polishing and her heart was very heavy with the thoughts of they're dying son at the radiation care facility located some one-hundred and fifty or more miles away. Jake was just walking into the meager kitchen when the wall mounted telephone rang out a startling voice of warning, which was immediately sensated by them both, as Cellia stopped dead while holding the can of polish in one of her old and shaking hands, while the cloth was in the other, and her aging eyes staring off into the hall leading into the kitchen. "Jake, can you answer the phone/" ,called Cellia worriedly. "I'm already here, Honey." ,Jake cried out. His heart pounding as he then picked up the receiver to answer it as an unnerving feeling stabbed at the man's very soul that was equally waiting and had been suddenly stirred into silence. As if time itself stood momentarily still, Jake answered the telephone, and he heard one of the physicians explain what has happened to they're son. Suddenly, by Jake's reaction, Cellia walked hurriedly into the hall and immediately into the kitchen and rapidly grabbed the free hand of her husband. Jake said, "Oh, my God; no…..We'll be right there as soon as we can." Cellia thought that Nuke had died and she yelled, but Jake calmed her temporarily experienced fears about the ending of Nuke's life. He told Cellia that Nuke had finally fallen into the coma this morning, which was about two hours ago, and he was in no pain as morphine was being steadily administered through his PICC line and that he was not suffering, but they were to come to the facility anyway to sign papers as well as to visit him if they wanted. Jake told Cellia to pack they're bags while he made reservations for the hotel so they could be there for Nuke.

Cellia was writhing in her emotions and crying like a child, but her soul cried out unto the God she taught her son about when he was so very young. Her very heart was bursting out at it's seams as she could not bare this any longer, but she was still unable to accept, although she knew she needed to, to say her final farewell. On the trip to the facility things were completely silent and even a bit foreboding, as if entering a trip into another plain of existence, which was likened to where they're son was now headed in only a matter of days. They passed the "Sequoya" nuclear power plant as it was seen in the distance which measured about one of two-hundred yards away from the roadside. A unanimous and completely tacit set of emotions crept over this older couple as they stared at it's often ominous presence that was now more like a sentinel of hate and affliction, rather than a repository and distributor of energy. Jake's eyes were filled with rage while his wife's were full of a softer form of the same feeling, but unknowingly hers went deeper than her husband. The pick up truck they were driving towards they're distant destination seemed to feel they're very thoughts and feelings as it drove them along this road that was almost inevitable not to pass by.

Before the Wilcox's saw they're son, they were now in the family room with the thanotologist Kathleen as she explained the necessary things to them about paperwork that needed to be taken immediate care of. However Cellia was crying as she asked her about Nuke's coma. Kathleen explained that he was in absolutely no pain and that all of his physical and medical needs were being constantly taken care of. Jake was stronger in the realm of his seething emotions, but his wife was soon to feel the intensity of her concealed "nuclear bomb" or "warhead" as she went to visit Nuke in a short time from now.

They entered the room of Nuke, and Cellia cried aloud as she cared not if anyone here heard her, but Jake also was taken back momentarily at the sight he was now seeing before him in this rather small room containing a nuclear victim-his son.

Nuke was still lying here in his electric hospital bed in the usual position with his right gnarled arm bent and a bit outstretched, while his paralyzed left arm, the one containing the PICC line inserted into it, was in the same place as it too sat atop the bedding that was a bit more so he would be warmer. The oxygen was also the same, but what was the redundant feature here? It was the fact that Nuke looked so shriveled up; like a little old man, which was exactly what Cellia, his mother, had remarked through her painful cries. Jake, her husband, definitely agreed with this sad, but stark statement. His mouth opened a few times, and this did not startle them, but rather reversed they're once sorrowful feelings back into hope and potential, as Jake jumped up from his chair and yelled frantically for a nurse to come to the room. A nurse immediately heard the plea for help, so she raced down the dark hallway into the room belonging to Nuke. "What is it?!" ,the nurse asked worriedly, her senses alerted for a probable procedure to help him, but no. They told her about Nuke's mouth moving open and closed on occasion. She checked and saw it. The couple saw it too and said frantically, "See!—did you see it?"

"Yes." ,replied the nurse kindly and even sadly, "Nuke is all right; it's completely normal during comas. He is swallowing his saliva and just moving his mouth, as this is very common. In some people it is barely seen, but more so in others. No one really knows why, but I assure you, Nuke is fine and he is absolutely no pain." "He looks like a poor shriveled up little old man." ,cried Mrs. Wilcox tearfully, "My poor Nuke; all from his radiation sickness." "I know." ,replied the kindly nurse compassionately and somberly, "I'm so sorry. You're son has given us all great joy and it has been more than a pleasure to know him" All was again silent, save for the medical equipment here in this room.

Cellia, Nuke's mother walked over to her comatose son and gently stroked his bald head over and over and kissed it, as she went further down to his once badly burned cheeks from the raw nuclear waste coming into full contact beneath his lead lined suit when it spilled. Her warm tears which were spilling from the woman's eyes, gently rolled onto Nuke's face and top of his bald head that was also badly shriveled from the terrible and unspeakable affects of nuclear radiation. She talked and said to him, "I love you, Nuclear....My little baby;

my little Nuke…..(Sob, sob)….Why God did he have to get radiation sickness?-WHY?" She suddenly broken down and embraced her son as he continues to lie there unresponsive. Her husband came over to her and wrapped his right arm around the woman's quivering back as it stridently writhed up and down. "Cellia, Cellia…,"Jake tried to gently cut in to get her attention, "Cellia, Honey. Nuke can't hear you; at least that is what they told us what kind of coma he has….I love him too, and there is nothing we can do; it's up to God now. In a few days he will be gone from us. You've got to let him go…..oh, God…Nuke." Jake was also overcome by what he saw as he continued holding his wife who was so distraught and eschewed in the seemingly dyer realm of her grief that was ever ticking away as the warhead was getting set to launch. Cellia watched her son's mouth gently motion open and closed as his head moved momentarily to their direction, which was to his left. They had been told these are some of the things that are seen by certain patients who have slipped into comas. However it was so surprising as it was even "wonderful" to experience for this grieving couple.

Each day they returned and visited him, but in between this, doctors who examined Nuke, felt a stronger pulse and a more steady heartbeat---This was not possible!

Dr. Henkel, although an anesthesiologist, was also a wonderful physician who cared exclusively for Nuke like Dr. Pierce who was a Professor as earlier mentioned. Dr. Pierce was called in to see Nuke's strengthening vitals as it was discussed as a very possible conclusion that the man was hearing what was being said to him, and his parents were there for a very long time the previous day. Nuke's mouth opened up completely into a very wide circle as if in a dentist's office, but of course, he was not. He opened his eyes while in the night, but of course, Nuke was still in his deep coma, as this can happen and is very common, although it is still under extensive research and study as to just why this happens, as the human brain is still a secretive mystery that is solely God's creation, and His alone! Nuke was taken down to M.R.I. while in this said comatose state, as he was only in it for not even two days, and they were seeing things that should not really be for a patient in his particular condition. Nuke's brain was severely damaged from the deadly and destructive effects of the highly lethal exposure to nuclear radiation from the accident at the plant. His brain's hemispheres, especially the cerebellum, was badly destroyed, and appeared to have been gnawed at, but it was as said, from the extensive radiation poisoning. Nuke would obviously never wake up, but they wondered if he may be possibly hearing things going on around him after all. He was watched when his parents entered the room to visit and talk. It was recorded by a nurse and physician, namely Dr. Pierce, with the permission of the parents, which Nuke actually reacted to Cellia's gentle touch and voice. Jake, on the other hand, felt inhibited and remained in the distance as he only sat there in one of the chairs near the bed, but against the wall as his head could be perfectly seen through the lead glass window as the green curtain was open now that the patient was in this tragic state. Nuke only opened and closed his mouth over and over again, but he did not do anything further, save for the opening of his mouth into a wide circle and he kept it this way for several hours.

When the medical professionals left the room of they're son, Jake and Cellia held each other and cried together and forgot where they really were as a way of forgetting it, repressing what is happening. They just wanted Nuke to be free as this was also finally admitted by his wife. The stillness of death was creeping in closer and ever closer to these people who were his parents. The night spent together in the hotel room that was only four miles away from the nuclear victim care facility was like an eternity to them, but in relation to the living soul it was not. The darkness of the night caused them both to huddle even closer together side by side in the king sized bed as the only thing that could be seen was the red light on the digital clock. However they both were obviously hypnotized or mystified by what they saw the other day, and nevermind the initial day when this same couple entered the room that was completely dark. Yes, the whole place knew he, Nuke Wilcox, was actively dying right now, and there was only a matter of days. But the following morning, something happened to this couple that they will probably never forget.

They received a phone call on Jake's cell phone that was eternally turned on, and they hi-talied it to the facility. Nuke cried out!—but it was only a dream—a dream drempt by Jake Wilcox, as he awoke in a glistening and dripping ocean of sweat. He cried to his wife Cellia as she woke up and immediately questioned what the matter was. She wondered if Nuke had died, but no. Jake was crying and shaking excessively as he reached out desperately, and even fearfully to his wife who he knew would be a great assistance to him. She, also sweating herself, embraced her husband who was quivering in fear. He reached for his silver cell phone, a very expensive cell phone worth $450.00 with mirrors all over the inside and was made by "SAMSUNG," and the service was provided by "VERIZON." The darkness of the night and the hotel room could not deter Jake from finding it, as he somehow knew where it was kept on the nightstand by the bed and the clock with red glowing numbers. He flipped it open and called the hospital and asked immediately fro the nuclear victim care facility, and he told them it was an emergency. Amidst the quiet of the room, Cellia and Jake stared at one another in an embrace of terror as each held his breath. He found out that Nuke was fine, but he had cried out! They asked Jake how he knew this?-did someone call him? "No." ,replied Jake quietly and subduedly, "I guess I just drempt it....I'm sorry to have bothered you...bye." He flipped the cell phone closed and gently held it in the grip of his hand, as Cellia also heard what the doctor said at the other end of the wireless line. Her eyes also bugged themselves out as had those of her husband. They held each other in the intense pitch darkness and stared at the unending night, or rather into the darkness of they're very souls; or into the darkness of DEATH.

Nuke's condition had sustained itself for a few more days past the suspected "cut-off" date that would mark his death. They remained by his side and talked to Nuke in a loving manner, as Cellia had even told her son that he looks like a poor little old shriveled man. She hugged this pathetic comatose soul that was her only son who once worked in a nuclear power plant and had slowly and insidiously died form advanced radiation sickness, but he had somehow still remained living. Jake held his son's hand that contained the implanted PICC line as it was delivering T.P.N. and his fluids combined with morphine to quell the terrible pain, which he was not in any at this point in his life. He looked so peaceful, which was exactly what both of his parents said to each other over and over again while sitting here by his side. He was, and

Nuke soon finally passed away, but fortunately he was not by himself, as even if he had been, he would never be alone, as God is surely with him, especially this man with an affectionately nickname, "NUKE."

When Nuke finally died, Cellia screamed bloody murder as all of the nursing staff, who was free, raced immediately into the direction of Nuke's room. They found the poor shriveled man, who's body, akin and bones, and limbs that were completely gnarled and twisted, and his parents crying over him. He was at peace and no longer suffering from the terrible affects of the industrial accident that happened eighteen months ago at the famed "Sequoya' nuclear power plant in the state of Tennessee.

The memory of they're only son will never be forgotten as will his recorded words taken by both the media, and the 'Department of Energy," or "DOE."

"NUKE" :'No. The spill of the nuclear waste didn't really bother me, but it was the pain…uh ha…I really miss working at the power plant, but I can still see my friends who never forgot me. Even the "Department of Energy" sent me a card will all of their names on it. They are nice people who helped my folks and me, but still I kept telling them not to worry, as it was all my fault. It was just a stupid thing; an…accident. That's all it was; an accident. I fell into the nuclear waste; no one else."

FRIEND; "The nuclear power plant is not the same without him. We all miss "Nuke," but we know he is still with us and we can call him as well as se him, which is a blessing indeed."

FATHER, Jake Wilcox; "Nuke's laughter is as innocent as he is. His strength, I believe, gives us strength to carry on each day. Every time I drive by that damn power plant I just go cold and numb inside. I think of the nuclear waste sitting there inside of the repository and how, because of a faulty robot weld, now my wonderful loving, and kind son, innocent as innocent as could be, lies in a facility for his advanced radiation sickness which he will eventually die from, and knowing that every time I turn on a light, watch the television, use my tools, or do whatever I need to do that uses electricity here, I think of our son as he was almost killed right there from some negligent fuck who didn't program the robots properly that weld the lids of these barrels shut. Nuclear waste....(Sigh)....my wife and I can't leave this town we've been living in all of our lives, but everything electrical is generated by nuclear power all around the adjacent areas too. "Nuke" was right, when even as a kid he told me that the nuclear age is going to eventually be the wave of the future, Dad."

The death of they're only son was a peaceful one, although how they felt as parents was far from being anything in that category. Nuke was peacefully here in his comatose state and suddenly ceased breathing, yet there was a gentle presence experienced by them both immediately following his demise. Jake and Cellia Wilcox were very tearful, but it was his wife who screamed and embraced her now deceased child. She caressed his face that was so emaciated, and shriveled, and gray from the eighteen months of unimaginable suffering as a survivor of a nuclear accident, as he was so badly damaged from it, and from especially the radiation, that nothing out there would be able to stabilize or save him. However the Wilcox's knew once he had fallen into this coma, Nuke would quickly reside to his Heavenly destination. The radiation care facility would surely not be the same at all now that Nuke was gone form them, as all people who worked here had gotten the wonderful chance to truly know him, and even to love him, but this was achieved by taking constant care of him. Nuke in turn returned his appreciation to them all, and regardless of how much pain he was in, which included that of the psychological. The signs stolen from the power plant were removed and tossed away, but Cellia, Nuke's mother, removed them from the trash basket in his darkened room that was now completely quieted of the sounds of medical equipment like his feeding pump, or I.V. pump, and the oxygen. They kissed Nuke's bald head, but had quickly decided to perform this same showing of true love and affection on his face, as he now could no longer feel the tremendous agony from the nuclear waste as it made contact with his skin all of those months ago. Neither one of them really wanted to let him go, but it was inevitable and the correct thing to do. However, that figurative warhead of Cellia's suddenly detonated itself. Meaning after the funeral that

for it all to go into the body via an intravenous. I remember I was firstly diagnosed with "Chronic Fatigue Syndrome," but it was not. I had not the strength to lift my head for weeks, as I slept almost twenty-four hours a day for a long, long time. I couldn't tube feed as I threw up continuously and my hair fell out in the doctor's hands, which was a heaping handful, as it was my guess the count of hairs was about fifty. I looked dreadful and I grew steadily thinner and thinner, as I had no energy and I was listless unendingly.

Surprisingly when I was informed by my compassionate physician I had radiation sickness, I only shed a moment of tears, but then I remember I was not worried as this is a part of life, I told myself. But again, it was the idea of receiving no medical help was what drove my emotions into a short lived nose dive as it made things harder to bear in this light of reasoning. As said, I was wasting away to begin with, but more so later as my thyroid began to not act accordingly until the age of thirty-four, then it all abruptly ceased as if nothing happened to me in the first place. Thyroid storm occurred very frequently and although I contended with it every way possible, I was diagnosed with the above condition then sent home, and I returned to bed unable to rise and simply patiently waited to die. I repeat-I waited to die-like so numerous other published and not published instances, but certainly no matter how one looks at it, it all falls under exactly the same criteria as something literally atrocious and completely unfair and highly benidictive of a misguided form of hate, as it is simply because most care not about things as these. However tales of medical atrocity like mine were published long ago and again and again, but all on an intermittent basis, as it was due to me as the author, and all carried out painfully for the whole reading world to copiously see and to take into themselves, but I as this same author has always noticed with an alarming amount of gravity, that many similar stories are being published, heard, and talked about freely all over the overcredulous media circuit.

I often angrily cry to the Heavens, "What the HELL is going on??!!!"

The biological effects of radiation vary drastically, particularly those concerning ionizing radiation as it interacts with living tissues by transferring energy from it to cellular structures, but by means of the latter, which again is transferring the radioactive energy into the molecules, which redundantly means that cellular functions may thusly become impaired either on a basis that is temporary or permanently as the result of this mentioned action. In fact, the severity of the injury specifically depends on the type of radiation, does of absorption, the absorption rate, and the radioactivity of the living tissues involved via exposure, ingestion, etc. However the overall effects are the very same, whether it is from a radiation source outside of the body, or has been ingested and taken inward.

The biological effects of a large dose of radiation that happens to be delivered at a rapid pace great differ from the same dose that is delivered to the body slowly. The effects of radiation delivery are widely known to cause cell death, as this affliction becomes apparent in only hours, days, or even weeks, depending greatly on the above. Protracted exposure is better tolerated as some of the damage is repaired although the insidious exposure continues, and even if the total dose of the radiation is relatively high, as it was in my case prior to getting radiation sickness. However if the said dosage is sufficient to cause severe and acute clinical effects, then self repair is less likely to occur.

But again as in my case, exposure to radiation too low to cause severe damage to the body can actually induce cellular changes that can be detected many years later. (Although my particular case of radiation sickness was considered as mild, it was still severe concerning it's overall clinical effects, and changed many things for me, as new and completely different manifestations erupted, especially concerning not only my thyroid, but my bone marrow, although always defective concerning it's natural ability to absorb iron, which it has never been able to do, is now failing every once in a while, and transfusions are a must to retain my already failing life.) But it's severely acute effects, which are usually high while body doses or radiation produce a very characteristic pattern of medical injury to living tissues and organisms. Doses are normally, in the U.S. are measured in rads, which translate only to a shortened term for radiation, i.e. low rad nuclear waste. I rad is equal to an amount of radiation that releases 100 erg's of energy per gram of matter. However doses of more than 400 erg's can severely damage the human vascular system, which at times can cause cerebral edema that can lead to a profound shock and neurological disturbances as death can happen within a period of only 48 hours upon exposure. Whole body doses between 1,000 to 4,000 rads can cause less severe damage to the vessels, but this leads to a massive loss of fluids and precious electrolytes within the intercellular spaces as well as the gastrointestinal tract, as death can happen within a lapse of ten days due to such loss of fluids and electrolytes, as severe damage to bone marrow can also manifest during this interlude, which can lead to infection, hemorrhage, and even death, but again if this should happen, demise of the body can happen in a few weeks. Only lower doses of radiation, ionizing in nature, can be effectively treated, but if untreated, people receiving as little as 300-325 rads to the bone marrow will die.

Exposure to small areas of the body, like medical situations, etc, which is the most frequent type of radiation accident, always leads to localized damage to tissues. When these same areas of the body's blood vessels are exposed there is damage to blood flow, which always causes disturbances in organ function and in higher does of ionized radiation, necrosis, which is death of localized tissue that leads to gangrene. (The spore known as clostridium perfingens that causes gas gangrene, and is well known in my prior field of mortuary and embalming.)

Injury to the body from internally ingested radiation substances is not likely to cause acute effects, but rather a delayed phenomena, and sharply depending on the "target" organ as well as the substance's half life as radiation characteristics and biochemical behavior of the radiation's source. These sources can not only be ingested in nuclear medicine like myself, as in nuclear isotopes that decay immediately, due to their uneven or abnormal atomic number of neutrons, hence the glowing that is seen during this certain type of scanning, which is characterized by a green or even yellowish glow, or as in the case of power plants, gasses, which are easily inhaled, or in the case of a powder that can be transferred easily into the mouth.

There are also nonmalignant delayed effects of ionizing radiation which are manifested in many human organs, particularly in bone marrow, the kidneys, lungs, and the eyes, which can cause cataracts, as in my case also, by degenerative alterations and functions which become increasingly impaired, as these are largely secondary to damage of blood vessels. However the most important "late effect" of this kind of radiation, nuclear in origin, is an increase malignancy as cancer rapidly inhibits the cellular cycle, but at a much faster rate and with striking ferocity. Like in the story, the victim's cellular structures were rapidly breaking themselves down, and this is also an added terror in which must be considered, but this is highly rare to be seen, hence not much is known further than what little scientists and physicians have so far acquired after years upon years of intensive study and hypothesis. However as one who has always studied this fascinating subject of nuclear radiation myself since I was at least the age of nine, it has certainly come as to no surprise to me in regarding this above medical information, as well as the tragic fact that this same author who had thusly brought it to the reading audience had come down with the same affliction we call "RADIATION SICKNESS."

In the pages of this very heart touching story, although is rather short concerning it's span, certainly is a "tool" in the arms dump of the mind regarding the neglected part of the self, but just as importantly, and in some particular cases more so, the raw and poignantly stark statement of humanity today and it's ever changing regimen of values which are in the state of declination as they are of making a return, which is mainly because of the church and this new and vibrantly diverse era which exemplifies tolerance and innovation. But just what is tolerance?—not much, because it is really a kindly way of promoting this statement, "I am willing to put up with you." In this Professor's educated opinion, this is most indeed a very sorrowful way of promoting a positiveness, but at the same time, this word perpetuates a falseness regarding it's true meaning, hence fooling those who take loving heed in the above disclaimer. But the story itself which was just written, is also an exclusive and equally powerful manifestation of this author's very close and real experience with radiation sickness, but now along with a real terminal illness that is very rapidly in the process of finally taking away this writer's life; the feelings, the thoughts, and especially just what concerns just what we dying face inevitably each and every day until that final moment is thusly achieved. However what was truly manifested here in a rather redundant manner is the "love" this same author is barely at all experiencing, and regardless of the above statement that is tightly cradled in truth and an accompanying joyful form of sorrow. I am left out of life in a way that is highly criminal and should never at all be, especially where it should thusly concern my, (our) ,most vital needs, desires, and sorrows, as this list much includes my death that is finally soon to come. But the process and final destination of the young toxic waste worker in the prior story are all are all really my own as I had even possessed the very same bodily demeanor and facial characteristics as well as the bald head which manifested itself two completely separate times, but as the person I am I manipulated my illustrations to make this truly poignant story of a senseless tragedy come more alive to the senses of the reading audience. Still he was loved, appreciated, and even fiercely assisted by leading officials and legal officials whose only mission was to help this poor suffering victim and for him to receive some tangible form of compensation for all of his torturous suffering. Yes; his suffering!

I speak very candidly and informatively about radiation sickness in a poignant manner, because of not only the fact of myself succumbing to it at one time, but I wanted to equally create a very memorable impact, as well as a point that there exist people scattered all about this ever changing world as these people are suffering and dying left and right from this copiously sad, disease, or rather affliction, or man's desires to ever alter his environment as he is now doing more harm than then aiding it. Many nations, especially that of Russia, formally the U.S.S.R., India, Canada, and of course, the United States, have the most nuclear power plants in the world and reserves in stockpile of plutonium, as now Korea is soon up and coming, especially with the major fall of Communism. However the conceptual process of nuclear power has certainly been both the subject of out right ridicule and often an irrational form of panic, but again, there is always the consistence of human error as he makes often lethal mistake while amidst these so called changes to better ourselves and our ever increasing demands for energy or whatever else he indiscriminately wants as he equally rarely takes precedence and responsibility for his failures. But, are we really?

No. Again, it is this very serious subject concerning that of human error and even downright stupidity, and this is where a manmade nuclear environment is thusly mentioned in this commentary, because there are victims of this same environment. Although I was a victim of radiation sickness, and suffered tremendously form the effects of it for approximately two full years, I was again one of the very few fortunate ones, although my premature aging has been placed into high speed and now my bone marrow, although is highly defective, has grown into a worsened state and even terrifying condition just as my thyroid, but even that was something which had been luckily self limiting, or self repairing, until the mentioned condition abated at the age of 34.

The story with the title of a condition, "RADIATION SICKNESS," or an effect of this ever changing environment, will surely and most definitely make others think long and hard about those hidden individuals who are tremendously suffering form it and it's lethal or devastating effects. As I said in the passages of this same story, "These people have a certain facial appearance that is highly benidictive of just what they have gone through, and once it has been seen, these faces are surely never forgotten."

But in this same story that is as heart touching as it is revealing, the young victim still maintained a sense of true gentleness and patience in the direction of his unprovoked enemies, which were those at the very nuclear power plant where he worked so happily, and even joyfully, for twenty-one years of his life. Again, it is the subject of his compassion towards his enemies as well as his caregivers while in the nuclear care facility, as it never seemed to evade his truest of personally conceived intentions. He never blamed the place that, in his eyes, gave him life; a chance at hope for a brighter future in a rural place, but still candidly holding onto the past in which he has grown. Becoming completely ravaged from the terrible effects of the high level of nuclear radiation, and rom the industrial accident in which he fell prey, "Nuke" Wilcox, this toxic waste worker, still somehow managed to keep himself peacefully aware of not only the ultimate consequences of their mistake, or inexcusable blunder that should never be forgotten or done again, his very soul swam daily in his personal sea of peace which comes only from endlessly following God, and only God. He touches people everywhere he had gone, but more so since his succumbing exclusively to advanced nuclear radiation sickness and becoming so severely ravaged as he plainly gave in joyfully to his slow and stead journey to his death. Even when this same damaged man was informed that he was going to lapse into a coma just days before finally dying, Nuke's mind, heart, and very living soul, accepted this news and sighed with an overwhelming feeling of an unconditional ecstasy as he was joyously aware of the promise that surely awaits him, as he subconsciously anticipated the end to his suffering, or being 'nuclear," as this poor victim preferred to call himself, as it is a term in which he derived, as had this author, when he was so radioactive he was in quarantine for seven weeks as no one could go near him or be in the same room without a lead lined suit and a geigercounter.

Again this gentleness in which fervently is attempting to make itself known to the reading audience; this is the dominant theme here that lurks so mystically and openly within the character of the book. As a woman of faith, of God, there perpetually exists the unending desire to expiate these so vital emotions and lessons attached to these said emotions, which have been so graciously given to us originally by Christ Jesus; our only Lord and Savior. Another adjacent topic equally comes into full circle here in this commentary, and it had everything to do with nuclear energy, nuclear weapons, and peaceful uses, etc. It had taken place in 1987, and I was painting in the kitchen of my home in Middleboro, as I was only the age of twenty, but as known form previous books, a very learnnerd person for one so young. The religious order known as the "Jehovah Witnesses" which I do not really care for personal reasons, but we are all God's children nonetheless. I invited a young man and woman who were dressed in their plain everyday garb and there was a young boy along side of them. They handed me a pamphlet about the subject of nuclear war, and the end of the world prematurely by man's nuclear weapons, and there was a very viable question printed on the cover; "Is earth really on the brink?"

I was asked if I feared nuclear war, and I told them both with a tidal wave of utter certitude and glory, that I have never once believed that God would allow his children to purposely destroy the world He has created for us as well as Himself, as accidents have happened, but I have not once feared or believed this would ever occur. Tears were literally rolling from the eyes of these two wonderful young people as the boy accompanying them was completely silenced. I had a smile of joy on my face as every beat of my heart was for His love and Eternal word which spawned all of creation. They both explained to me that in three months they have been submitting these pamphlets personally and asking the very same questions, and not one of them answered like this, as they all clutched fear rather than joy and truth. It was I, Milkweed, who taught them something that day, which was surely witnessed as it was received; but certainly not by me, but by God.

But returning to the main character known only to the reader as 'Nuke," however he was "Nuclear" to his mother Cellia Wilcox. The family, but in particularly his parents, continued to cottle and reveal to him on a daily regimen just how deeply they're love went as these people advocated endlessly and tirelessly to acclaim not only what happened to they're son, but most equally and in sense of contrast, and with depthful warrant, the utterly travistic behaviors and subversive conspiracies which plant officials made the gentle and shy man appear to be in the eyes of not only those nearest him, but to anyone else who may have read something about him and would thusly see the allegations that were ludicrous as they were overcredulous and bizarre. It is with the utmost credibility and justifying certitude that I, not only as a victim of radiation sickness, but including the above mentioned agenda, that I tell it all as it really happened, (i.e. the Beth Israel Hospital incident of terrorism in Boston, Massachusetts in 1996.), and in a manner of genre` that is completely devoid of fear as well as finally facing and feeling the so called "consequences" as all leaders, in some form, always face in some varied way. Victims are usually ignored from a worldwide perspective, but it is certainly with my well and formally educated opinion as a Professor of religion as well as a theologian, only those said victims who are cared about in a "genuine" fashion, or those with whom the public sympathizes truly make the news at all, and nevermind those who have no sense or understanding of what happened to them. But how can anyone, and in any nation, no matter how impoverished or how rich, can completely and repetitively ignore, and regardless of the pending situation?

Myself, Lama Milkweed L. Augustine, a Ph. D ;one who has received my Doctorate of Divinity in the Buddhist faith, which is extremely difficult anywhere to achieve, and nevermind how young I was upon the time of finally receiving it, which had been the age of twenty-eight. All are aware, or if not, made so by myself or by means of my books which are dispersed throughout the world, about the utterly inhumane and gruesome forms of terrorism which I had been solely a victim here, unbelievable forms of mistreatments, and of course, prolonged famine that was forced and sustained, and torture, which once again had all taken it's place right here under their noses in the United States of America. I spoke to the masses everywhere possible and was strictly commanded by God to walk the streets and to gently inform about the hidden plight that is well concealed from the eyes of the generalistic masses, which is the hated death penalty and changing peoples' obviously viewed and heard misconceptions one person at a time, and using what happened to me only as something to strike a cord of a powerful form of nonconformism and a manner of inner comprehension that when once it is achieved, can rarely if ever, be taken away from those who now clutch it.

To place this summarization as bluntly as this activist and religious leader does to her readers and to those who see me speak; "Man can take no precedence upon himself, as there is only one God, and we must listen to all people just as He has heard us."

There most certainly are no substitutions for compassion, but as I am saying this last statement regarding me, I truly want for the reading audience to take these words deeply inward and mold them to one's individual faith based understanding, and perhaps become illuminated in the process.

"I, Lama/Catholic Milkweed L. Augustine, say these words to all: It is not necessarily the media or the fault of the public entirely as to why this endlessly happens concerning anything about me. It is because I am literally nothing just as we all are, but certainly everything to God. Yet I am beyond the meaning of nothing, hence the very pulsating reason that is painfully loitering from beneath the cloak of not compassion and protection, but rather of a form of apathy which rivals the worst of hypocrisy, and even complete prejudiced hate which claims no glory, but by that to Satan." Amen

Although things in this commentary may sound unappealing and even "Marxist" to some readers, it is most certainly with a deep respect that is entwined with my mentioned educated opinions in relation to our great nation. However it has finally been acknowledged in somewhat of a miniscule manner, and some of this realization has been withdrawn from "my" many books and reviews, that torture does exist in the annals of America, and right now. People have retrieved my e mail address from databases as well from World Trade Centers, which are not only here at home, but from the globe abroad, as most either ask for my caring assistance to fight for the rights of others like myself, or while some merely acknowledge me as a survivor of brutality and torture. Now with the help of from the book and the wondrous internet, I, Lama/Catholic Milkweed L. Augustine H.H. Ph. D., will endlessly reverberate a lasting impact and personal form of impact in the lives of not only those who ask of me, but this includes those who don't. I am known by the 14th Dalai Lama as can be seen in the ending of my first full length book publication "Eternal I.V. Pole" Copyright 2003. (Authorhouse, formally known as 1st Books Library in Indiana.) I have been lovingly embraced as had my greatest work 'The Milkweed Prophesy; Epitaph of the Apocalypse" by the Oblates Missions of Our Lady of the Immaculate Conception here in the U.S. in an abundant manner as they not only faithfully return their prayers, but expressions of sheer joy and very personally felt elations from receiving the book in which I had given to them as what God had thusly petitioned for me to do in His precious name, as this same book truly was, 90% of it, written by God, Jesus Christ, and by our Blessed Mother Mary, as this too has been felt, avidly and honestly believed and sensated exclusively by fellow people of the cloth as they shudder, because they feel the very "breath" in which these highly prophetic and very truthful words have been spoken through this living conduet-Milkweed L. Augustine H.H. Ph. D. I have carried the blessed crucifix in the beloved church in this forested town of Middleboro, known as "The Sacred Heart Catholic Church of Middleboro." All, at first, reached out to literally touch my sleeve of a part of my person, the sleeve of the alb which was made exclusively for me following the Mass, as like any other instances, wearing my gold pectoral cross attached to the glorious Pontifical cord, and a very old fiddleback chasuble which I collect as a woman of God: As if truly sensating the "Saint" which has been eternally loitering from within, which was thoroughly entailed in the book.

Speaking of the book, "The Milkweed Prophesy; Epitaph of the Apocalypse," since it's initial date of final date of publication in June of 2006, it has been sold, sold, and sold-just as Mary said! (It was sold within the first two days of coming off the press.)

Others' personal lives have changed in ways which could not be explained, however in my next book entitled "Songs of Milkweed; A Gift From the Fields Volume 2," there will be glorious photos of the above entry as well as book signings I had set up, which were to benefit my fellow terminally ill adults for a wonderful organization which is known as "The Dream Foundation" and is based in Santa Barbara, California. However like the story just read, these stark and ever sorrowful photographs of myself lying in a hospital bed away from home and receiving a life saving blood transfusion consisting of whole blood as I was literally dying that very day, and like a "saint," I sang and mysteriously drew people into my room as I had no neighbor, due to me literally being in critical condition. These certified nursing assistants who knew me, and also those who had not known me, heard my gentle and joyful voice humming that very sacred song which will be played by bagpipes at my funeral that is son soon to come; "Amazing Grace."

They all heard me and learned what was really happening. Later my gentle and ever loving earthly mother, Marguerite Augustine, was here at my side as was the staff and the Clergy. I sang in Latin and prayed some in Latin, and held out my arms and so joyfully welcomed death of the finite body as I once again saw perfectly and without blemish, our Blessed Mother with whom I have known since I was restored of my lost physical sight as the age of only eight months. My mother saw her very first apparition of Mary! Praise be to God! She wept and so did I as I waited as did Mary, for the final word from God to carry His saint back home. I remember I felt the Holy Spirit literally "hit" my heart as I momentarily leaped like the time when I experienced a massive heart attack and was shocked, but this here was not it, as I thought immediately of Pentecost as that Holy Spirit descended with flaming wings of glory and entered the disciples as well as that of our Blessed Mother Mary in the upper room at Mt. Zion, which was across the street from where Mary lived. I was in ecstasy unimagined and I literally attempted to physically go aloft towards the "love of my life"—to God. With outstretched and wasted arms that bared a PICC line my soul accompanied the unimaginable glory of our one God, His Kingdom and it's truest form of proclamation, which is one of the glorious mysteries of the rosary. My bone marrow that is scanty had failed and had not been working at all for a period of three days as I had ceased forming white blood cells, or known as leucocytes and they were rapidly disappearing as hardly and red blood cells remained as well. It had later been spoken to me at the hospital about me receiving a bone marrow transplant, but like all good and truly worthwhile things in my already traumatic life, and pertaining exclusively to me only, I am barely, if ever, a recipient, hence receiving constant transfusions. Myself as well as genuine specialists wonder along side me if this affliction, which has grown worse, may have remotely been due to me having radiation sickness although it had occurred long before. Still I have always had defective marrow as no fatty, or yellow marrow, exists as it cannot absorb iron at all and it equally cannot hold it as a means of reserve when not being taken into the body just as the precious amino acid known as hemoglobin, which gives blood it's red color, used to fall to dangerously low levels, as the carrier of iron in my blood sometimes gets so high, if I had not had diseased marrow function, I would have surely died as this is very lethally toxic to the body. I even experienced the beginnings of "total endocrine failure" as it was documented at "Good Samaritan Medical Hospital," once known as "Cardinal Cushing" as it is located in Brockton, Massachusetts. I have a copy of this document and sent it to the "Mass. Board of Registration in Medicine" in Boston when I provided abundant medical information, including my terminal lung disease which I was "blessed" with, which more than anything, proved this hospital's downfall, as well as so many other falsified files they conveniently transpired to make real and known to all as LAW.

Here amidst the pages of this interpersonal commentary, which is also being the subject of manipulation as a cipher for my agonies and profoundly witheld grievances, there yet exists a sense of varied complexity that surely plagues us all who have suffered in this particular light, but in particular, "radiation sickness."

Although in the beginning, upon finally being diagnosed correctly, I barely received care, however it had been later when I finally underwent a scant degree of ethical treatment comprised with medical treatment by my doctor—the physician who I lovingly mentioned by name with his permission prior to his untimely death in the book "Eternal I.V. Pole"—Dr. Stephen Merrill. He administered a type of Quaalude for the gut wrenching nausea that is associated with the tragic disease that in most cases is self limiting, or can eventually heal itself in a relative dormancy. The cure of radiation sickness is varied depending upon the degree of bodily exposure as well as the type of radiation that is taken in.

Although there exists no method of care which can reverse of effects of radiation poisoning, the said treatments are mainly for the care or for the symptoms and to alleviate suffering to a degree. Although antibiotics are used to treat the lowered immunity of patients, I myself was not the recipient of any, but later I succumbed to pneumonia, hence I received them. The subject of anemia comes into play here as well as blood transfusions in this case are administered, but I am forever in this condition and before this state ever coming to me, hence this was ruled out although the condition eventually worsened over a short passage of time. Drugs approved exclusively by the (USFDA) "United States Food and Drug Administration," for radiation contamination by means of an industrial accident, which is like the man in the story, or what is sometimes known as a 'dirty bomb," may include Radiogardase, Pentelate Calcium Trisodium, (Ca-DTPA) ,and Pentelate Zinc Trisodium, (Zn-DTPA). In fact, it is not well know by the general public that these specific drugs are held in stockpile in case of an emergency, which brings to light the terrible accident that happened in the story to this young man.

Radiogardase, also known as Prussian Blue, or Prussic Acid, which is also a mild derivative of cyanide, can be used to treat patients who are exposed to radiation which contain high and or lethal amounts of Cesium-137 or thallium. Ca-DTPA and Zn-DTPA can equally be used for contamination with forms of radioactive plutonium, americium, and calcium, as all of these above mentioned drugs are used to alleviate or eliminate, or even to draw out, radioactive substances from the body.

There yet exists another specialty drug that is administered to fellow patients, but mostly to those who have been exposed to high doses of radiation is called 'Filgrastin," (Neuopogen), which is also used in normal medical circumstances for people under chemotherapy. This very same drug just mentioned, is also used to stimulate growth of while blood corpuscle, or leucocytes, and help repair damage to bone marrow. However this same drug had been mentioned to me by my hematologist last year following this priorly told "brief" about the time when my defective bone marrow had completely failed for a total of three days, but as said, nothing further transpired for the good of me. But if the cause of radiation exposure is unknown or consists of more than one source, like what had happened to me in reference to being exposed to more than one source, a combination of drugs may be used to either prevent or to treat radiation sickness.

Yes, the above brief outline and explanation pertaining to actual care was not mine, save for the literally destructive and even "crippling" nausea. But in this story in which the reading audience, by now, has gained a better comprehension of such medical horror and tragedy, however, it is this one main character called Mr. "Nuke" Wilcox who becomes the narration; the story itself.

I realize as the author, it must be difficult to wrap one's self around a rather repugnant situation, especially where one possibly becomes a bit desensitized due to such a world we now live in. But I honestly and firmly believe as a woman of God, and as a fellow human being, no mater how caught up we may become with particulars, such as war, events in politics, terrorism, etc, etc, there most avidly and eternally exists a special little place deep inside that is that is specifically reserved for the caring of others, as well as FOR others. It is called the "human heart," and when that heart, so caught up in matters of the above, should suddenly see a soul who has been victimized, but more so likened to the manner of the above and in the story as something reminiscent of a transcendence begins, because these very special victims in all of the criteria that is known as medical, silently reverberate a silent but loud outcry of our very realistic fallibility in which we all face. There is surely a lot to be said about the folds of truth's "cloak" as the same idea which ever festers in the timeless realm of lies which have been conjured up strictly by the medical world. However in the reaches of this same heart warming story, lies and deception flourished, but unlike the real life of the dying author, they perpetuated and pursued me like the Devil and his entire unholy and infernal realm.

I wanted to avidly and chronically bring to light a relative number of things to the reading audience which throb eternally beneath the surface as someone who has fallen sure prey to our modern world; "RADIATION SICKNESS."

There are overwhelming complexities in the many things I have said both here in the prior story which exemplify just what I think and what I most redundantly believe in a tireless manner, which is far from being considered as a facquade, and exactly how and why I feel the ways I do about my own death and the ever worsening condition. The pensive notion and highly realistic conception of knowing God up close and personal is a definite must for all of we human beings, as we are all in His beloved image; body and soul. Our desire to love, to heal, and in a select view, "to pick up our crises and follow Him." It is true and equally sad to me that so very few of my fellow dying never come anywhere near to my defined and acclaimed sense of having an unconditional love of death, the acceptance of death, and the ever increasing frailties and declination of the fallible body that becomes our "container" for a brief moment while upon the earth. The Catholic tradition known as "Ash Wednesday,' the first day of Lent, as I receive the blessed gift as a it serves as a chronic reminder and testament towards and acknowledgement of the fact that we shall become ashes once more as we had priorly been, which is so extremely benidictive of the circle complete-the Alpha and the Omega-the beginning and the end.

"From ashes to ashes, from dust to dust," and "From dust where'st ye made, and dust ye shall be."

Amen!

"Nuke," although well aware he had a rare fatal form of radiation sickness, and because of the situation, and told he would die a horrific death, smiled quietly with his eyes that although were filled with tears, were expressing a very realistic joy in a belief that dwelled so deeply inside of him since he was a small child. Yes, "Nuke" was a child, but an adult, who lovingly embraced the Godhead in a rare manner that was constant as it was recurring and with the same clamoring at the blessed feet of Christ had gotten this damaged man much more than an acceptance of what has thusly happened to him and just how he will deteriorate and die, but equally 'Nuke's' very soul epitomized his very belief system by means of living out his suffering in Christ, and finally dying in Christ.

The coma that had befallen this kind and truly gentle peace loving man had not graced him with any means of fear or of anger, but an automatic acceptance of it as he smiled, and in his blood laden eyes, which was a common effect from the nuclear radiation that was killing him so insidiously expressed something truly glorious in which absolutely no one could mimic; not even the greatest actors in the world or of all time, because these silently expressed ideas, thoughts, and emotions, can only erupt into a person from the

Kingdom of our only Lord God; our Father.

There exists a genuinely felt form of coming together in the teachings of our dear and precious Lord Jesus in the lives of not only those who are dying with no cure lingering on the horizon, but equally for those who had been imprisoned like myself, as well as all of those who dwell in a different kind of the former term, as this same author has made so numerously clear in my past words of wisdom. Please never even begin to make an attempt to underestimate those who withold a flower of glorious and very realistic faith, and concerning those who are not in danger of losing life in a purely physical perspective.

As I earlier mentioned, although most of my fellow dying barely, if ever, come to this relatively "sacred" state or anywhere close to it, wither bodily and spiritually, which in essence is a tragedy, which is in a way, as bad as the condition of "Nuke" Wilcox, the nuclear toxic waste worker in the previous narration, because the spiritual health is really just as vitally important to receive it's reconciliation with it's ever loving and solacing Creator. For this is something within the young damaged man had already secretly known,

As it should be known to us all.

In the final installment of this rather striking commentary produced by the author, it is important to break away momentarily from the spiritual, but only to make the reading audience comprehend some brief explanation about the nuclear industry, but in particular the nuclear power plants and nuclear wastes which inhabit not only our country, but within those other particular world powers in which I had earlier spoken.

First of all, nuclear power plants generally have three types of radioactive, (ionizing) ,

Waste treatment and handling systems for both the processing and then storing the low-level waste that accumulates as part of normal procedures and operations. These said systems treat as well as store the liquid nuclear waste, which concerned with this type 'Nuke" Wilcox had fallen with while manually transferring, and there are gaseous radioactive wastes, and of course, there is solid nuclear waste.

The "liquid" radioactive waste systems are used to collect, to process, and finally to store liquids from any source, which are sumps in potentially contaminated areas as the containment, auxiliary or reactor building, and turbine buildings. (BWR) a type of water reactor.) There are also systems which collect radioactive leakage, but there is normal discharge which exudes "from" cooling systems or reactors, (e.g. during starting.) or other systems which are connected "to" reactor cooling systems. (e.g. pressure relief tanks) or are located in potentially radioactive contaminated areas.

Typically these liquid wastes are thusly collected in large storage tanks. The liquids are then processed by means of using ion exchangers to remove both radiation and chemical contaminates. Water that meets chemical criteria (e.g. chlorides, fluorides.) can be reused. However if not, it all may be reprocessed. However water which does not actually correspond to regulatory criteria, specified in "Title 10 Code of Federal Regulations Part 20" can be discharged into the environment. Chemical and radioactivity levels within these storage tanks and process streams are always monitored via samples taken. Again, if criteria in not met, the water can be routed through additional ion exchangers. In some nuclear power plants reverse osmosis units can be used. At one specific time, evaporators were used to both purify and to process water, however, experience shown with these mentioned units only revealed they were too expensive to run, and were susceptible to heat exchanger tube leaks, and were insufficiently able to properly process the quantities of liquids in a nuclear power plant.

The radioactive waste liquid systems are used to provide makeup to reactor cooling systems, chemical and volume control systems, emergency core cooling, and finally, spent fuel storage pool.

There are two most used forms of "water reactors," which are "light" and "heavy" water reactors. A variety of reactor types, which are characterized by the kind of fuel that is required , the moderator and the kind of coolant used , have been built throughout our world for the production of electric power. In the United States, and with few exceptions,
Power reactors use nuclear fuels in the form of Uranium Oxide that is isotopically enriched to approximately 3% uranium-235. The moderator and coolant are really highly purified water, is no ordinary water. A nuclear reactor like this one just briefly mentioned
Is called a light water reactor. (LWR)

In the "pressurized water reactor" (PWR), which is really another version of the LWR, the water coolant operates at a pressure of 150 atm and is pumped through the reactor's core where it is heated and to a temperature of 325 C, which is about 650 F. The superheated water is then passes through a steam generator where steam is thusly produced to drive, or motion, one or more turbine-generator systems.

The reactor pressure vessel is about 15 m (49 ft. high) and 5 m (16.4 ft). and in diameter with walls measured 25 cm (10 in. thick). The reactor core houses approximately 82 metric tons of Uranium Oxide which is contained, or encapsulated, in thin corrosion resistant tubes, which are placed together into tightly packed fuel bundles.

In the "boiling water reactor," (BWR) which is also a second (LWR) the water coolant is allowed to boil within the core, and by operating at a relatively low pressure.

The steam which is produced directly inside of the reactor pressure vessel is used to drive, or motion, the turbine, as no external steam generator is need in this particular industrial

Application.

The level of power in an operating reactor is generally monitored by a variety of thermal, flow, and nuclear instruments. However power output is generally controlled by either inserting or removing, from the reactor core, a group of neutron-absorbing control rods. In fact, the position of these said rods actually determines the power level at which the chain reaction is self sustaining.

During operations as well as after shutdown, a large 1,000 megawatt (Mw) power nuclear reactor contains within it, billions of curies radioactivity. However radiation that is emitted from the reactor during it's operation, and from the fission products, splitting of atoms, which follow shutdown is then absorbed into thick concrete shields around the reactor and it's primary cooling system. Yet there are other safety features included besides the one just mentioned, which include emergency cooling systems for the reactor's core, that prevent overheating in case of malfunction of the main coolant systems , and a large steel and concrete building to retain any radioactive elements that might try to escape from the nuclear reactor in case of a leak.

Although there was well over 100 nuclear power plants that were either being operated or built here in the United States, and at the beginning of the 1980's, in the following tragedy of "Three Mile Island" in 1979, concerns regarding safety and economic factors which were in combination, were in essence, and manipulated to stop further growth in nuclear power. And there were no further orders to build nuclear power plants since 1978, and some of these plants that were already built during that time, were not allowed to operate. In 1987 about 16 % of electric energy in the country came from nuclear power plants, as in France, well over half the energy being generated was from nuclear power plants.

In the early 1950's, the initial period of nuclear power development, enriched uranium was available only here in America and in the U.S.S.R. The nuclear power program in Canada, France, as well as Great Britain, literally centered themselves around "natural uranium reactors." In this type of application ordinary water cannot be used as the moderator, because it absorbs too many neutrons, which carry a neutral charge. However because of this limitation, Canadian engineers developed a reactor coolant and moderator by means of deuterium oxide (D_2O) or what is more commonly known as "Heavy Water." The ten reactor CANDU system satisfactorily operated, and because of this achievement, plants of this type have been built in India, Argentina, just to name a few.

However in Great Britain and France, the first full scale power nuclear reactors were fueled with natural uranium metal rods, graphite-moderated, and cooled with carbon dioxide gas under a specific amount of pressure. These initial designs have been stopped by Great Britain, but by a system that uses a fuel of enriched uranium. However in France the initial type of reactor that was chosen was also stopped in favor of our, U.S., PWR design, where enriched uranium became more readily available from French isotope-enriched power plants. Russia, or previously the U.S.S.R,. has a large nuclear power program that uses both graphite-moderated and PWR systems. (pressure water reactor)

In the world of manmade nuclear power there yet exist other kinds of reactors which are possibly not known by the public masses. There is another kind of reactor called the "Propulsion Reactor," as nuclear power plants that are similar to the PWR are used specifically for the propulsion plants, or large surface naval vessels like aircraft carriers, but the basic technology of the PWR system was first created and developed here in the United States of America naval reactor program by Adm Hyman G. Rickover. In fact, reactors for submarine propulsion are similar from a physical perspective and use more highly enriched uranium and is smaller to permit a more compact reactor core. America, Great Britain, Russia, and France all have nuclear powered submarines with these above power plants.

There is yet another type of nuclear reactor called the "Research Reactor" and where a small variety of nuclear reactors were built in many nations for training, research, as well as for the production of radioactive isotopes fro industry, agriculture, and of course, nuclear medicine. (One of the contributing factors as to how I received radiation sickness.)

These said reactors generally operate at levels of power at only 1 MW, except at more major national nuclear development programs.

There is a type of this reactor being used in a frequent fashion and is called the "swimming pool type." The core of this reactor is generally made of partially or fully uranium-235, but it are contained in an alloy of aluminum plates and then are immersed into a large pool of water that takes the place of both the coolant and the moderator. The neutrons which are produced in this kind of reactor are absorbed by the appropriate materials to produce radioisotopes, or they are merely allowed to leave the reactor in special beam tubes for experimental purposes only.

The 'Breeder Reactor" is certainly another reactor that is not widely known by the public masses, and I will explain. Uranium, the natural resource on which manmade nuclear power is based, i.e. put to use by man, although it has always existed and produces radioactivity, occurs in dispersed places throughout the world. The total supply of this naturally nuclear substance is not known and it may be limited unless very low concentration sources, such as granite and shale were to be used in this field of industry.

In a conservative forecast, U.S. resources of uranium having a cost which is acceptable, lie somewhere in the range of 2-5 million metric tons, but the lower amount of this natural element could support an LWR (light water reactor) nuclear power system that provides 30 % of electric power in the United States for only about a total of fifty years.

However the principle reason for the brief life span of the LWR nuclear power system, is it's very low efficiency in the usage of uranium, as only approximately 1 % of the energy content of this uranium is even made available in this particular system. The main feature which lie in a breeder reactor is that is produces more fuel than it consumes. The reactor does this by promoting the absorption of extra neutrons in a fertile material like uranium-238. Technically several breeder reactor systems are considered to be feasible. In one type of breeder reactor, thorium is the "fertile" active material, as it is transmitted by neutron absorption in a reactor into uranium-233, a fissionable isotope of uranium which is similar to the natural uranium-235. The breeder reactor system that has received the most attention worldwide uses uranium-238 as the "fertile" material. When uranium-238 absorbs neutrons in this type of reactor, it is then transmitted to a new fissionable material, plutonium, through a nuclear process known as B (beta) decay.

In the process known as beta decay, a neutron reactor decays into a proton and a beta particle. When plutonium-239 absorbs a neutron, fission, or the splitting of atoms, can easily manifest, and on the average aproximity about 2.8 neutrons are released from this process. In an operating reactor, one of these neutrons is needed to cause the next fission to keep the chain reaction going. Generally speaking, about 0.5 neutron is lost by absorption within the structure of the reactor or in it's coolant. The 1.3 remaining which are left can then be absorbed into the uranium-238 to produce more plutonium through the reaction firstly briefly explained. (i.e. (beta) decay.)

The breeder system that has the greatest development effort is called the "Liquid Metal Fast Breeder Reactor (LMFBR). In order to make the production of plutonium-239more productive as well as maximized, the velocity of the neutrons that cause fission must remain fast, which is either at or near their official release energy. Any moderating materials that may slow the neutrons must be removed from the reactor. For this reason water cannot be used as a coolant, rather a molten-metal, liquefied sodium, is the preferred liquid coolant. Sodium is used in this particular application, because it has good heat transfer qualities and melts at about 100 degrees C (212 degrees F.) and it does not boil until the temperatures reaches at least 900 degrees C (about 1,650 degrees F). However like anything, it has it's drawbacks, which are it's chemical reactivity with both air and water, and the extremely high level of radioactivity that is induced in it within the reactor. Development of the above reactor, or called the LMFBR, began in America before 1950 with the first construction of the very first experimental prototype breeder reactor, EBR-1, it was called.

A yet larger program of this type on the Clinch River was stopped dead in it's tracks in 1983 as only work pertaining only to experiments was to continue unevaded. In the countries of Great Britain, Russia, and France, working breeder reactors were thusly built installed and maintained as experimental work continued in Germany and Japan.

In one particular design of the Liquid Metal Fast Breeder Reactor, LMFBR, nuclear power plant, the core of this reactor consisted of literally thousands of stainless steel tubes which contain mixed uranium and plutonium fuel, which consists about 15-10% plutonium-239, and the remaining uranium. There is a region which surrounds the core of this type of reactor is what is known as "breeder blanket," which contains similar rods filled with only uranium oxide. (oxidized uranium) the entire core and blanket assembly measures to about the dimensions of 10 ft. high, to about 16.4 ft. in diameter and is supported by a very large vessel which contains molten sodium that leaves the reactor at about 500 C, or at 930 F.). The vessel also contains the pumps and heat exchangers that assist in removing the excess heat from the core. In a second sodium loop steam is finally produced, and is separated rom the radioactive coolant loop by means of the intermediate heat exchangers within the reactor's vessel. The entire nuclear reactor system is housed within the confines of a large steel and concrete containment building, as this also acts as a protective shield in case of radiational leaks.

As spoken from a mild point, the LMFBR produces about 20 % more fuel than it consumes. In a large power reactor enough excess new fuel is produced 20 years to allow the loading of another very similar nuclear reactor. In these LMFBR's about 70 % of the total energy content of the natural uranium is made readily available as it contrasts to the 1 % of the light water reactor, or the LWR.

This following explanation in a narrative format talks exclusively about some of the 'behind the scenes" of the previously read story that is based on non-fiction, which is the subject of nuclear waste, which is the element, besides the excessive amount of nuclear radiation absorbed by this man's body, and is also known as the "Nuclear Fuel Cycle."

Any power plant that generates electricity is really only one part of the total energy cycle. The nuclear fuel cycle includes many steps, and in the United States uranium is mined and the ore that is concentrated in scattered mines in the western states. The concentrated uranium ore is then shipped to a conversion plant where it's chemical form is changed into uranium hexafluoride gas, UF, which is the "freed" material from an isotope enrichment plant. In the conversion plant, natural uranium containing 0.7 % uranium-235 is then separated into two streams, which one is enriched uranium to 3 % uranium-235, while the other is a more depleted stream-the tails-which contain most of the original natural uranium that is now at a concentration of only 3 % of uranium-235. The "tails" stream is stored and the enriched product is sent to a fuel fabrication plant. While there, the enriched UF gas is converted into uranium oxide powder, then made into ceramic pellets that are loaded into corrosion resistant fuel rods, as these are then assembled into fuel elements and are shipped to a nuclear power plant.

A typical 1,000 MW "pressurized Water Reactor" contains about 200 fuel elements; one third are replaced every year, due to the depletion of the uranium-235 and the build up, or residue, of fission products caused by atom splitting, (fission) ,as the absorb neutrons. At the end of it's life within the nuclear reactor, the fuel is tremendously radioactive, which again is because of the fission products in contains and hence it is still producing a very considerable amount of energy. The discharge fuel is then placed in water storage pools at the reactor site for a year or more. At the ending of the cooling period the spent fuel elements are thusly shipped within heavily shielded metal casks either to permanent storage facilities or to a chemical reprocessing plant where the unused uranium and the plutonium-239, produced inside of the reactor, are recovered and the radioactive wastes become concentrated. In the 1980's no such facilities were yet made available in America for our power plants' fuel, hence only temporary storage was used during that specific period.

The spent fuel still contains almost all of the original uranium-238, which is about 1/3 of the uranium-235, and some of the plutonium-239 that is produced within the reactor. In cases where the spent fuel is sent into permanent storage, absolutely none of it's potential energy content is used , but in cases where the fuel is reprocessed, the contained uranium is thusly recycled through the diffusion plant and the recovered plutonium-239 may be used in place of some uranium-235 in new fuel elements.

However the low use of uranium in the LWR, light water reactor, is evident from these fuel cycles. In the "Open Cycle," most of the "freed' uranium only ends up in the tails stream and in storage of waste. Even within the "Closed Cycle," where the uranium-235 and plutonium-239 are recovered and finally reused, only about a simple 1 % of the total uranium energy potential is used. The fuel cycle in the LMFBR must be a closed one, because the plutonium "bred" within the annals of the reactor is recycled for reuse in new fuel. The feed to the fuel element fabrication plant consists of recycled uranium-238, depleted uranium from the isotope separation plant stockpile, and part of the newly recovered plutonium-239. No additional uranium needs to be mined, as the preexisting end tails stockpile could truly support numerous breeder reactors for a count of literal centuries, which again is because the breeder nuclear reactor produces more plutonium-239 that is requires for it's own refueling, which is about 20 % of the recovered plutonium is stored for later usage in starting up new breeder nuclear reactors. Because new fuel is "bred' from the uranium-238, instead of only using the natural uranium-235 content, about 75 % of the potential energy of uranium is made more available by means of the breeder cycle.

The final step in any of the fuel cycles is the long-term storage of these highly radioactive wastes, which remain biologically dangerous for literally thousands of years. There are several types of technologies which appear satisfactory for the safe storing of nuclear wastes, until most recently, there were no large scale facilities that had been built.

In the 'Open Light Water Reactor" fuel cycle, the fuel elements would either be shielded or stored in guarded repositories for later and final depositing. However in the closed cycles, the concentrated wastes would become converted to very stable compounds, fixed in both ceramic or glass, and encapsulated in stainless steel canisters and buried far underground in very stable geological areas, like "Yucca Mountain" in Nevada.

Public concerns for the safety about nuclear power from fission comes from two most basis features in the so called system of criteria. The first is the high radioactivity level which is present at the various stages of the nuclear cycle. The second one is the fact that uranium-235, and plutonium-239 are the materials from which nuclear weapons are manufactured. President Dwight D. Eisenhower had announced the "Atoms for Peace Program" in 1953. It was perceived as conception of a future cheap, but plentiful energy in copious amounts. The utility industry hoped that nuclear power would eventually replace ever increasing scarce fossil fuels, and by doing so, would significantly lower the cost of electricity, as these same groups, as well as those more concerned with the environment, equally hoped conserving our natural resources foresaw a massive reduction of air pollution and strip mining. Amazingly the public, in general, looked upon this new energy source, by seeing the transitional change from the use of nuclear power from weapons of war and mass destruction, for use in peaceful purposes. After the short lived excitement about this proposed Presidential plan, the public then grew very concerned and as their reservations concerning nuclear energy grew, greater scrutiny was thusly given to important issues of safety and nuclear weapons prohibition in not only the United States, but equally in other countries as many groups still oppose having nuclear power and the regulatory process has now become very complex as it is vexing and often highly confusing. For example, Sweden has limited it's programs to only 10 nuclear reactors, while Austria has terminated it's nuclear program indefinitely. While in complete contrast, Japan, Great Britain, France, and Germany are continuing uninhibited.

The safety of the nuclear power reactor has been the recipient of the most attention and for obviously for all of the right reasons. In an operating nuclear reactor, the fuel elements contain, by far, the largest fraction of the total radioactive "inventory." A number of barriers prevent fission products, which are classified as nuclear wastes, from leaking into the biosphere during normal operation. The fuel itself is enclosed inside of corrosion resistant tubes, as the heavy steel walls of the primary coolant system of the PWR, or the "Pressurized Water Reactor," only forms a second barrier against this. The water coolant itself absorbs some of the biologically important radioactive isotopes such as iodine, while the steel and concrete building that houses the whole system is yet another barrier; a third.

During the operation of a power reactor some radioactive effluents are released inevitably. The total exposure to those living nearby is generally only a few small percentage of the natural background radiation. However major concerns still aspire from radioactive release which is caused by accidents concerning fuel damage and where safety devices fail. The major damage to the integrity of the fuel is a loss of coolant accident in which the said fuel is either damaged or even melts. From here, fission products are then released into the coolant, and if the coolant system is breeched, fission products enter the reactor building. Reactor systems rely on elaborate instrumentation to monitor their condition and to control the safety systems which are used to shut down the reactor under abnormal circumstances. There are also back-up safety systems which inject boron into the coolant itself to further assist shutdown are all part of the PWR design and is standard.

Light water reactor plants operate at high coolant pressures. In the event of a large pipe break, most of the coolant would only flush into the steam and core coolant would be lost, but to prevent a loss of reactor core cooling, reactors are provided with an emergency core cooling system that start to operate automatically at the beginning of coolant pressure loss. (The moment it is sensed, the core coolant flows into the core.)

However in the event of a steam leak inside of the containment building, which would be from a broken primary coolant line, spray coolers are activated to condense the steam and to prevent a dangerous rise in pressure from entering the containment building.

The reprocessing of fuel step certainly well poses a combination of what is called radiological hazards, like the accidental release of fission products if should occur in chemical equipment or within the cells or the building housing it. There is also the chance of the routine releasing of low level, or inert radioactive gasses xenon and krypton. However the technology to provide a safe and efficient operation of a chemical reprocessing plant is most definitely a feasible request as it is a must for the overall safety of our planet and ourselves, but there still does not exist a plant like this in the United States.

In chemical processing there will always exist a primary concern, which is the separation of plutonium-239, which is considered as a material used in nuclear weapons. The tremendous dangers of it's surreptitious diversion, or intentional but well hidden production for the manufacturing of nuclear weapons is better controlled by political as opposed to technical means. With the improvement of security, which has most definitely been achieved, but especially in the most sensitive points of the fuel cycle and expanded international inspection that is carried out by the "International Atomic Energy Agency (IAEA) are the ones who surely offer the best prospects of controlling dangers of the diversion of plutonium.

The final step in the fuel cycle is, of course, nuclear waste; the very thing that re-created the main character in the story, it's management still remains one that is highly controversial. The main issue concerning nuclear waste is not necessarily that of the present danger, but more of the danger to those people and wildlife in the future. Many forms of nuclear wastes remain highly radioactive for thousands of years and are well beyond the spannage of any great institution or empire. The ever changing technology for packaging nuclear wastes so they pose no threat to living organisms, which naturally well includes our environment. The difficulty mainly lies with being truly competent and confident that those in the future are protected and that they too can make the correct political decision as to place the waste for storage and to retain that knowledge of caring for it. Permanent, but retrievable storage within deep and stable geological areas appears to be the most favorable decision at present. In 1988 the American government chose a site in Nevada called "Yucca Mountain" with it's thick section of porous volcanic rock as the nation's first permanent nuclear waste storage facility, or better known as a waste repository.

There is yet another vital span of information which has everything to do with the previous story just read, and that is the truth about an independently controlled agency that, although works alongside the government, it still is an independent entity, and it is called the "NUCLEAR REGULATORY COMMISSION." This entity was primarily established to regulate civilian nuclear activities. The "Energy Reorganization Act" of 1974 had completely abolished the once existing Atomic Regulatory Commission (ABC) and then transferred it's regulatory responsibilities to the NRC, which is the priorly mentioned institution, who's headquarters was in Bethesda, Maryland. All so called developmental activities then became combined into a new energy research and development administration altogether. In 1977, this finally became known as the "DEPARTMENT OF ENERGY." The Nuclear Regulatory Commission's programs are basically designed to protect the health and safety of the public at all times, to preserve the overall quality of our natural environment, and to protect nuclear materials from theft or from diversion, as mentioned earlier, and nuclear facilities from sabotage , and of course, to assure conformity with U.S. antitrust laws. These programs include standards and regulations, safety reviews, and licensing actions, technical studies, inspections and enforcement, and research in safety.

This is considered to be a truly major load of responsibility of the Nuclear Regulatory Commission in regulating the use of nuclear energy to generate electricity in nuclear power reactor plants. The activity of these specialized programs also include regulation of most of the nuclear fuel-cycle; from the milling of uranium, through their chemical conversion, the fabrication into fuel elements, use in nuclear reactors, reprocessing, and finally transportation to final storage and disposal of the nuclear waste. Outside of the fuel cycle, the NRC also regulates a wide variety of radioactive material uses in industry, commerce, agriculture, medicine, and education.

(Nuclear Medicine is partially the reason as to how and why I received RADIATION SICKNESS, and now with late effects, which I have recently found through another Boston medical hospital, my terminal illness is a combination of what I was born with, and the late effects from having radiation sickness. i.e. failing bone marrow, severe vascular disease that is so bad, regular intravenous cannot be used anywhere in my dying body, the wasting disease which I was also born with, has been made worsened to the point where I will die in a matter of days without my T.P.N. as this theory has been avidly proven in a hospital setting as I was lapsing into a coma in less that a week without being intravenously fed.)

"RADIATION SICKNESS."

The author,
Lama Milkweed L. Augustine Ph. D

"Some Final Sentiments"

ALTHOUGH THIS STORY IS filled with many great tragedies, there is yet a great deal to be said regarding to what we human beings call "faith." Faith is the reward which is given to us directly from God by following Him and when one is willing to endure those things in earthly life that are so often the most negative of all. Faith is also the cause for healing and for transitions; to lower one's self in hope of knowing our only Lord and Savior, and with that mentioned hope, comes the promise of exultation , which is by humbling one's very self.

Religious faith, like so briefly mentioned above, can never be confused with having it in others, as we are always let down in some form or another, but having an unconditional faith in God, His only Son who is precious, who is Jesus the Christ, the friendship of the Holy Spirit, and ever looking up to our Blessed Mother, Mary ever virgin, we as human beings who have been mirrored in their glorious image, can find this invaluable emotion and perception that is most surely intertwined with an understanding, in essence, can never be taken away-even when all is truly lost to us-like in the tear laden pages of the story of this kind young man who slowly and surely died of a rare form of radiation sickness. This is what, I as the author, fervently wish to make understood just what can honestly happen when someone carries this faith deep inside of them. We as His children, like "Nuke," should cradle in an endless stance that glorious reality when intertwined in the fibers of the soul can do the impossible. Even in the part of the story when "Nuke" had been quietly informed by the thanatologist , or death counselor, that he would lapse into a brief coma just prior to dying. This poor man only eyed her with tears of a combination of a genuinely felt sorrow that is very human, but on the same foothold of contrast, graciously combined with an emancipating joy as he looked forever inward and saw his Savior before him. His heart, like the heart of the author, and with the same form of tragic affliction, tacitly sang a praise of joy that his suffering would be thusly taken and it would never return. Well armed with this knowledge given to us by the Eternal Words the Father in Heaven, His Holy and Divine Son, which He literally "handed over" to give us another chance, because I believe as Doctor of Divinity, Sacred Theology, and a woman of God, but certainly a lowly and worthless human being, that they both knew we as His people, were not entirely to blame for our sins, as we were first tempted in the Garden of Eden by the dreaded Serpent. But despite this terrible fact that is obviously infused with the most painful form of glory that will ever be known in the annals of human history, we still chose to sin, to sin, and to sin. But still, there exists God's truest people, and "Nuke" Wilcox was one of them, as just by "gently" willing to endure and to fight what was happening steadily to him on a day to day basis, and at the very same wavering instant, touching all who know him and were responsible for all of the constant critical care within the confines of the radiation victim care facility, that by never giving up on life, because our Jesus, our Lord and only Redeemer, had done this gladly for us and for our only means of forgiveness, because without that horrid crucifixion there certainly never could be.

I ever make an attempt, even in the terrifying and sorrowful midst of my harrowing life, to make well comprehended to the eyes of the reader, the truths about our one Lord that must be understood as well as used as a "manual" to live by,…and how to die. But the word, "die" only is by the bodily means, the purely physical. The living eternal soul, like that of the one who lovingly created us, enters a different state of existence, which is a continuation in our quest for the truth, which is God and only God. Death is very often a frightening and even terrifying subject to most of the human populous due to the realistic fact about it being a "place" that is unknown. But the is most certainly the point in this discussion where faith comes most avidly into play, as most of the human populous lacks a realistically acclaimed form of this so vital state and truth, because it is a precious "commodity" that most of us either refuse to take it into our own lives, or just don't believe strongly enough , hence as to why I tirelessly attempt to both depict and to teach my caring readers about the glorious and blessed "man," truly Divine and stainless of sin, but was sent to us "as' a sin; to atone for "ours." I call my readers "caring' ones, because it takes one who is of a positive nature to pick up these often highly controversial books of mine and to make a very genuine attempt to understand the often highly serious subject matter, the rare genre,` and of course, what happened to me in the clutches of this wonderful nation I call "home."

"Nuke" Wilcox, like me, is the one of the few of God's truly chosen people who, regardless of circumstances and agonies of the damaged body which houses the eternal soul, still and without the slightest form of rebuttal, joyfully lived and died in his horrific medical and bodily status as he deteriorated so rapidly from radiation sickness that was highly rare in nature, due to the equally rare circumstances that determined this poor man's remaining life. He found a very real and genuine happiness amidst an ungodly bodily demeanor and suffering that would make anyone beg for death. However, "Nuke' still joyfully anticipated, and without fear, that often terrifying state so many of us fear to tread, because of the lack of a truly fervent and everlasting religious faith . However "Nuke" cherished whatever time he left to him, although this poor and severely damaged man, from a tremendous poisoning of nuclear radiation, became so catastrophically destroyed and could never leave the facility that housed him as he required endless and chronic, critical care as no form of nursing and Hospice home could even know how to perform any type of medical care for 'Nuke," and not to mention, this man was so nuclear radioactive for the initial seven weeks following this industrial accident at the power plant, he was in "RADIOACTIVE PATIENT QUARENTINE" as only those wearing lead suits, breathers, and carrying geigercounters could go anywhere near him, and nevermind when he has to be operated on to save his rapidly failing life.

Imagine being so medically ill such as the above situation, that not even you're loved ones can come near to embrace—even of for the last time. I can as well, especially when the time arrived when I was going to have a bone marrow transplant, but even now in my present state, completely devoid of hair on my little head, I am happy and so joyful in anticipating the ending of my eternal suffering, especially following so many times when I have actually "crossed over" and achieved further miracles as they correlated exactly to all concerning what "they" have told me. But again, it is the "faith" I have in God and in the crucifixion and dereliction, as I hold this moment as eternally sacred as is it so horribly benidictive of the resultive action of our sins, as most of us would rather refuse to believe in a glorious and omnipotent presence who is alive and eternally loving, and desired to create us, and hence as well, and follow the opposing one who is literally the very embodiment of sinfulness and all things Godless, and inverted. How, oh how can this be?!! How can people like "us" i.e. "Nuke" Wilcox, the toxic waste worker in the story, and so many of us true believers, live in a world filled with relatively endless sin and repugnant horror? The responsorial answer is surprisingly easy to see as it is to known and to comprehend, and this is to endlessly acknowledge Him and to eventually "enthrone" Him, like our Blessed Lady who is seated forever at Christ's right hand.

Jesus said, "It is not you who chose me, but I who chose you."
Amen

There is also a very beautiful, but strikingly stark statement that Jesus said to Ponchos Pilate, the one who reluctantly sent Him to be crucified, and is surely something I know by heart, because it LIVES in my heart.

When the priests, or the Pharisees, wanted Jesus to be crucified for simply stating the truth; He is the Son of God. Pilate, the Governor for that district and ruled entirely by Czar, Pilate asked Jesus a question. Ponchos Pilate asked Jesus, "What sin are you guilty of; who sent you?"

Jesus said these words in answer to Pilate's final question,: "The one who has sent me, has done the greater sin." {His Father in Heaven had done this greater sin, because He literally 'handed over" Jesus specifically as the perfect sacrifice to abolish man's bondage to the first original sin and to free us from eternal damnation, censure, and death with no further destination other than simply wandering, etc, but instead gave us a Heavenly one by dying upon a truly wretched and torturous cross that is as infamous as the infernal realm of Hell.} Yes, Jesus even mentioned a glorious truth which pertains specifically to Himself as He proclaimed this prior to the crucifixion: "I am the only one who may resurrect myself." ,Jesus said.

These are just a few of the sacred things "Nuke" Wilcox held deeply in his heart, mind, and spirit, which this man carried within each day, hence here is the redundant topic of this discussion; "faith."

The poor young man suffered through the tortures of Hell as a victim of radiation sickness, but one who contained a rare form of it, due to the rare manner in which he achieved it. I believe with all that I have, that if man decided to, at last, proclaim a true faith in God, Jesus the Christ, and His truly infinite Word, and like the man called "Nuke," all would truly be saved, but not just concerning where he is going after death, but where we are going presently; to accept the otherwise unacceptable and to quell the agony associated so well with the human condition. When medicine fails to save the body, all is truly never lost when one clutches firmly the glory of God. "Nuke" Wilcox, the gentle man who's very existence was catastrophically decimated into nothingness, and he accepted what happened to him. He smiled often, because of clutching not only the above, but the child ever loitering within him. The man was wasting away in so many variances that it was impossible to not only save this poor man, but to even "repair" him, hence "Nuke" quietly remained her and called the facility his "home." He missed the nuclear power plant, which in this man's reddened eyes, gave him a life and a purpose, but it turned on him in an inadvertent manner. Still regardless of it all, this poor "little man" who shrank and shriveled into a mass of skin and bones, a living skeleton like the author, with gnarled and bent limbs, with a face as gaunt and gray as death itself, and a bald head that immediately told the seer his appalling testimony. "Nuke" certainly lost his abilities to speak, to think and to remember, to move, to function, to combat incoming illness, and finally to breathe and void bodily wastes, hence he peacefully passed away in the full and unobstructed presence of his loving and ever dedicated parents who had always loved him accordingly. The poor young man never blamed the nuclear power plant, or it's inexcusable blunder, that shook apart the entire U.S. nation and brought both the civilian/military nuclear industries and programs to it's trembling knees and begged for mercy. But again, "Nuke" this poor victim in the accident, never once became angered nor had he sworn vengeance on power plant officials as Nuke was purposely spared the completely disgusting efforts of conjecture and mercilessly battering his loving and quiet character as this truly would have mentally injured this poor damaged man indefinitely.

'Nuke" was a man of peace and not nuclear terrorism.

"Nuke" Wilcox sought the lowest place, even while working at the power plant, and received his genuine exultation in Christ, hence revealing his truly "gentle" and happy acceptance of the advanced radiation sickness, but this also well included his destination once it had taken it's full stronghold and from there dumped the final "payload" within and throughout this man's poor, wasted, and shriveled body.

As a survivor of a mild, but genuine form of radiation sickness, but now suffers from "late effects," I feel utmost strongly that this is my sole responsibility, in my final hour, to inform the world that is so criminally unaware of people who are in this appalling situation and tragic form of medical health which mostly leads to death. But also, to make a testament to those, who once again are unaware, but not because of ignorance, but as I stated a while back; the media, and fellow humanitarians and activists, the government, but not the Federal branch as much as the civilian. It is vitally important to the world, and for it to fully be able to comprehend these individuals, like me, who are purposely hidden from the collective knowledge of society, which lies in perfect accordance concerning my life of torture, purposely deprived of all that pertains to society and human contacts, life sustaining medical care, ethics in all phases and situations, and of course, the painful subject of education.

One may ask how I became a Professor. I certainly can explain, but the explanation would surely take a while as it was all highly unorthodox at best. However I surely am a self made woman, who by solely from the eternal grace of God, I was, at last, recognized affectionately by the Holy Catholic Church. Again the book "THE MILKWEED PROPHESY; EPITAPH OF THE APOCALYPSE," continues to alter personal lives of all those who read it, but it has been proclaimed universally to me as, "an extension of God's Eternal Word." (The greatest religious book ever written in our modern times.)

But in a humble bow, I once again prostrate at the foot of that glorious and triumphant cross. This "little Saint," as I am being called a lot now, joyfully awaits her promise; her personally achieved 'Calvary' that is soon to come as I have seen it just over the bend—Still fervently and genuinely there in my sights.

(Praise be to God.)

"Ver-voom Dominae`!"

Love the author

The Most Venerable
Lama/Catholic Rimpoche;
Miss Milkweed L. Augustine Ph. D   H.H.

www.ingramcontent.com/pod-product-compliance
Lightning Source LLC
Chambersburg PA
CBHW020918290526
45784CB00002BA/605